Get Ready for International Business

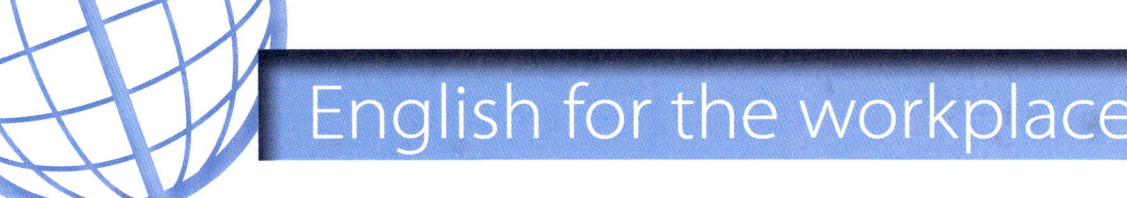

English for the workplace

A2

Student's Book 1

Andrew Vaughan
& Dorothy E Zemach

MACMILLAN

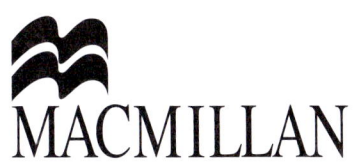

Contents

Page	Unit	Content
4	**Introduction**	
6	**1** Let me give you my card	Introducing yourself. Talking about your job Giving contact information Starting and ending conversations
12	**2** I start work at 8:30	Saying where you're from. Reflecting and reacting Describing routines Describing schedules
18	**3** What does your company do?	Giving information. Asking about company background Asking for repetition and spelling Describing company business
24	**4** How do you like your job?	Making small talk. Talking about likes and dislikes Making suggestions Sounding polite
30	**Review 1–4**	
32	**5** Can I take a message?	Talking on the phone. Answering the phone Controlling language Taking a message; ending a call
38	**6** Which ones should we order?	Discussing products. Describing and comparing products Understanding advertisements Softening language
44	**7** Are you free on Tuesday?	Making arrangements. Making a telephone call Checking information Making an appointment
50	**8** Where's the Marketing Department?	Getting directions. Prepositions of place Giving a tour
56	**Review 5–8**	
58	**9** How long does the process take?	Sequencing. Describing a process: sequencing; ordering a product; Checking and confirming Recruiting
64	**10** Exports increased sharply	Talking about data. Talking about graphs Giving a presentation Answering questions
70	**11** I'm leaving tomorrow	Confirming next steps. Talking about future plans Degrees of certainty
76	**12** Would you like to try some dim sum?	Entertaining guests. Offering and accepting or refusing food Giving and receiving compliments Thanking and responding to thanks
82	**Review 9–12**	
108	**TOEIC® or BEC practice**	
120	**Wordlist & Look it Up**	125 **Common irregular verbs** 126 **Grammar reference**

Viewpoints	In business	Talk business Student A	Student B
Using business cards	Your business card	84	96
Working hours	Describe your workday	85	97
What kind of company?	Describe your company	86	98
Corporate culture	Company survey	87	99
Mobile phones	Receiving and passing on messages	88	100
Advertising	Advertise your company	89	101
Using technology to communicate	Make an appointment	90	102
Workplace facilities	Give a company tour	91	103
Looking for a job	Design a process	92	104
Presentations	Give a presentation	93	105
Talking about the future	Describe future plans	94	106
Food and business entertaining	Planning a social event	95	107

1 Here are some of the companies and characters you will hear and read about. After the Viewpoints section in each unit, complete the information about each person.

UNIT 1

NAME Anna Martinez
JOB _____
FROM Venezuela

UNIT 1

NAME _____
JOB Student
FROM England | UK

UNIT 1

NAME Michael Yang
JOB Small business owner
FROM _____

UNIT 2

NAME _____
JOB Office worker
FROM _____

UNIT 12

NAME _____
JOB Product Planner
FROM _____

UNIT 12

NAME _____
JOB _____
FROM Argentina

UNIT 12

NAME Rajiv Das
JOB _____
FROM _____

UNIT 11

NAME Amnuay Chaichen
JOB _____
FROM _____

UNIT 10
NAME _____
JOB _____
FROM Ukraine

UNIT 10

NAME Mei-ling Chen
JOB Project Manager
FROM _____

UNIT 9

NAME _____
JOB _____
FROM US

UNIT 3
NAME _____
JOB _____
FROM Germany

UNIT 3
NAME Emiko Yamaguchi
JOB Banker
FROM _____

UNIT 4
NAME _____
JOB Civil Servant
FROM _____

UNIT 4
NAME Alma Hansson
JOB Accounts Manager
FROM _____

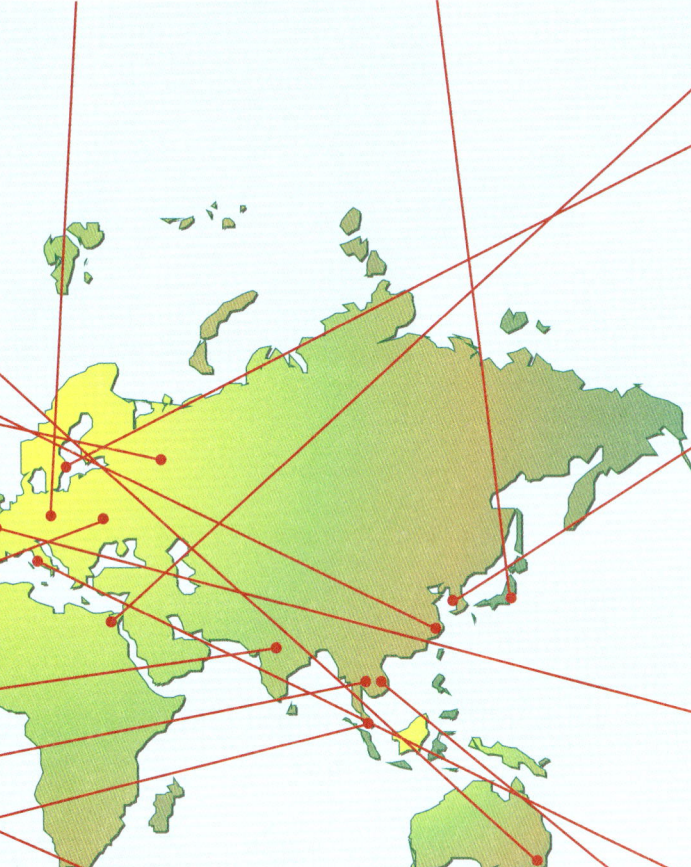

UNIT 5
NAME _____
JOB _____
FROM Korea

UNIT 6
NAME _____
JOB _____
FROM France

UNIT 8
NAME _____
JOB Marketing executive
FROM Brazil

UNIT 8
NAME Lise Martin
JOB _____
FROM _____

UNIT 7
NAME Tran Chung Nguyen
JOB _____
FROM Vietnam

UNIT 7
NAME _____
JOB Project Manager
FROM _____

Let me give you my card

Aims

- Introducing yourself
- Talking about your job
- Giving contact information
- Starting and ending conversations
- Viewpoints: Using business cards
- In business: Your business card

Listen and practise Introducing yourself

1 Describe the photo. Where are the people? What are they doing?

2 🔊 1.02 Sarah and Hari are meeting. Listen and write T for true or F for false next to each sentence. Then check your answers with a partner.

   a   They are meeting for the first time. _____

   b   They work for the same company. _____

3 🔊 1.02 Listen again and complete the conversation. Then practise with a partner. Take turns being Sarah and Hari.

Sarah: Hello. My name's Sarah Cohen. I ___work___ ___for___ Comet Technologies.

Hari: Hi, Sarah. I'm Hari Kumar. I'm _____ Asia Retailing. Nice to _____ you.

Sarah: Nice to meet you too. I'm sorry, I didn't _____ your _____ name.

Hari: It's Kumar. Here – let me _____ you my card.

4 Practise the conversation again. Change the information in blue using the names and companies below.

Josh Brown / Brown Construction

Su-yun Kim / Insung Limited

5 🔊 1.03 What do you think Sarah and Hari will do next? Tick (✓) your guesses. Then listen to see if you are correct.

   a ☐ Sarah will give Hari her business card.

   b ☐ Hari will ask for Sarah's phone number.

   c ☐ They will talk about their companies.

   d ☐ They will talk about their jobs.

Talking about your job

1 Look at the questions and answers about another person's job.
Ask and answer the questions with a partner.

A: What do you do? B: I'm (an Engineer). I'm in (R&D).
A: Who do you work for? B: I work for (company name).
A: Who are you with? B: I'm with (company name).
A: Where do you work? B: I work in (Berlin).

2 Look at the tables. They show ways you can talk about job titles and departments.
With a partner or group, add some more.

		Job title
I'm You're He's / She's	a / an	Web Designer / (Department) Manager / Product Planner / Researcher / Sales Assistant / Administrative Assistant / Accountant _____ / _____ .

		Department name
I'm You're He's / She's	in	Information Technology (IT) / Advertising / Human Resources / Marketing / Purchasing / Sales / Research & Development (R&D) _____ / _____ .

3 Complete the sentences using words from the tables above.

a He's *an*   b You're _____   c I'm _____   d She's _____   e He's _____
    Accountant

4 Listen to the conversation. Then practise with a partner.
Take turns being Amanda and Steve.

Amanda: Hello. Are you new here?
Steve: Yes, I just started on Monday.
Amanda: Really? That's great. By the way, my name's Amanda Parker.
Please call me Mandy. I'm an Administrative Assistant.
Steve: Nice to meet you, Mandy. I'm Steve Klein.
Amanda: Nice to meet you. What do you do, Steve?
Steve: I'm in Advertising. Well, I'll see you soon.
Amanda: See you.

5 Practise the conversation again. Change the information in blue using your own names and information from exercise 2.

Giving contact information

1 Look at the business card. Take turns reading the numbers and addresses with a partner. Then label the card with words from the box.

area code   country code   post/zipcode   at   dot   underscore

a _____
b _____
c _____
d _____
e _____
f _____

2 🔊 1.05 Listen to four conversations. Fill in each business card with the missing information.

Talk business
Student A, turn to page 84.

Student B, turn to page 96.

UNIT 1 Get Ready for International Business

Conversation strategy Starting and ending conversations

1   1.06 Listen to and read the conversations below. Which one is between friends? Which one is between people meeting for the first time?

Conversation 1

A: Excuse me. Do you have the time?
B: Yes, it's 11 o'clock.
A: Thank you. By the way, my name's Nancy Chen.
B: Nice to meet you, Nancy. I'm Mary Burns. Are you with Global Exports?
A: No, I work for Snappy Snack Foods. I'm in Marketing. Here, let me give you my card.
B: Thanks. Here's mine. I'm a Sales Representative for Golden Palace. We import Chinese food.

Conversation 2

A: Emily! How are you?
B: Hi, Liz. Really good. Have you heard that I changed jobs?
A: Yeah. Who are you with now?
B: Corporate Training Solutions. I'm in Human Resources. And you?
A: Oh, I'm still a Software Developer with Magix. I really like it.
B: Let me give you my new card.

2   Practise the conversations with a partner.

3   Look at these ways to end conversations. Which ones can be used with conversation 1? With conversation 2?

a A: We should get together sometime.
   B: Good idea. I'll call you this weekend, OK?

b A: Well, it was a pleasure meeting you.
   B: Good to meet you too.

c A: Anyway, I'd better get going. Tell your brother I said 'hello'.
   B: I will. See you!

d A: Well, I see someone I need to talk to. It was nice meeting you.
   B: You too. Goodbye.

e A: Well, my train leaves in about an hour. I'd better get going.
   B: I hope we meet again sometime. Have a safe trip.

f A: Oh, look at the time!
   B: Yes, I've got to go. See you around.

4   Practise all of the endings with a partner.

5   Choose an ending to conversation 1 and conversation 2. Then practise the complete conversations.

Viewpoints Using business cards

1 🔊 1.07 Listen to people from three different countries talking about business cards. Tick (✓) the sentences you hear.

Juliana Soares,
Student, England, UK

☐ I don't have a business card.
☐ Most of my friends have cards.
☐ Sometimes people give me their cards.
☐ I like fancy, colourful cards.
☐ I keep business cards in my pocket.

Anna Martinez,
Sales Manager, Venezuela

☐ I give and receive a lot of business cards.
☐ My cards are in English.
☐ I like plain white cards.
☐ It's important to treat cards with respect.
☐ It's OK to write on them.

Michael Yang,
Small business owner, China

☐ I have two different business cards.
☐ I give my card to everyone I meet.
☐ I give and receive cards with both hands.
☐ I like simple, clear cards.
☐ I organise them in a small notebook.

2 Discuss these questions in a small group.
- Which person is most like you (or people from your country)?
- Do you think business cards are important? Why or why not?
- Do you have a business card?
- How often do you receive business cards? Who do you receive them from, and why?

3 Look at these business cards in a small group. Which ones do you like? Which ones don't you like? Explain why. Use the vocabulary below and your own ideas.

(un)attractive   (not) easy to read   fun   (un)interesting   (un)professional   serious   simple

UNIT 1 Get Ready for International Business

In business — Your business card

Scenario: You and your group have been asked to design new business cards for your company. The company can be where you work, or where you would like to work. In the group, you each need to design a card for yourself.

1. Discuss in your group.
   - What is the company called?
   - What kind of company is it? Small? Large? International?
   - What does the company make / do?
   - What kinds of jobs are there?
   - What are the job titles of you and your group members?
   - What contact information do you want to include on the card?

2. Draw a picture of the company logo here.

3. Organise your information onto this card. Include your name and title. Each member of the group should make their own card.

4. When you have finished, introduce yourself to other groups in the class using your new business card. Meet as many people as you can. Remember:

   Introduce yourself
   ↓
   Ask them their name and where they work
   ↓
   Tell them your job title and where you work (exchange cards)
   ↓
   Politely end the conversation and move on

Let me give you my card UNIT 1

UNIT 2
I start work at 8:30

Aims
- Saying where you're from
- Reflecting and reacting
- Describing routines
- Describing schedules
- Viewpoints: Working hours
- In business: Describe your workday

Listen and practise Saying where you're from

1 Describe the photo. What are they doing? What are they saying?

2 1.08 Jeff, Beth and May are meeting in Singapore. Listen and write T for true or F for false next to each sentence. Then check your answers with a partner.

   a May and Beth are meeting for the first time. _____
   b Beth is from the United States. _____

3 1.08 Listen again and complete the conversation. Then practise in groups of three. Take turns being Jeff, May, and Beth.

   Jeff: Beth, _____ May Li. May is in Customer Support. May, _____ Beth Wild. Beth's a Designer for Star Design.
   May: Nice to meet you, Beth.
   Beth: Nice to meet you too, May. Where _____?
   May: I'm from Shanghai, in China. _____?
   Beth: I'm from San Diego, in the United States.

4 Practise the conversation again. Change the information in blue using the names and jobs below.

Kimiko Tatsuda (Nagoya, Japan)	**Maria Lopez** (Mexico City, Mexico)	**Mikel Deuter** (Essen, Germany)	**Lek Phikul** (Hat Yai, Thailand)	**Ben Poole** (Manchester, UK)

Marketing Assistant Hasegawa Hotels	Sales Manager BL Chemicals	Service Engineer Ruhr Pipe Manufacturing	Tour Guide Tour Asia	Product Planner Timson Watches

5 🔊 1.09 What do you think May will say next? Tick (✓) your guesses. Then listen to see if you are correct.

a ☐ Is this your first trip to our office?   c ☐ What do you do, Beth?
b ☐ How old are you, Bethan?   d ☐ Let me give you my card.

Conversation strategy Reflecting and reacting

1 Look at the table. It shows questions you can ask to reflect a question back to the speaker.

| What about you? |
| How about you? |
| And you? |

2 🔊 1.10 Listen to the four conversations. How do the speakers reflect the question?

a _____ you?   c _____ you?
b _____ you?   d _____ you?

3 Ask and answer the questions with a partner.

For example: A: *Where were you born?*
   B: I was born in _____. *How about you?*
   A: I was born in _____.

a Who is your favourite singer?   d Do you play any sports?
b Can you play a musical instrument?   e Where are you from?
c What kind of movies do you like?   f Do you like fish?

4 Look at the table. It shows ways you can react to information.

Wow!	Really?	That's a shame.
That's amazing!	That's interesting.	Oh no!
That's great!	I see.	I'm sorry to hear that.

🔊 1.11 Listen and repeat. Say the expressions the same way.

I start work at 8:30   **UNIT 2**   **13**

5 Practise with a partner. Take turns reading and reacting. Use the information below and your own ideas.

For example: A: *I'm getting married next week!*
B: *That's great!*

a   I'm studying French.

c   I lost my train pass.

b   I went skiing last weekend.

d   I have a bad cold.

Describing routines

1 1.12 Listen to May describe a typical workday. Next to each activity write how often she does these things. Then check your answers with a partner.

every day / most days / some days
once / twice / three times / four times /   a   day / week / month / year

get up at 6:30	a	*every day*
stop for coffee and a muffin	b	
leave home at 7:30	c	
have a morning meeting	d	
eat a sandwich at my desk	e	
study for an hour	f	

Talk business

Student A, turn to page 85.

Student B, turn to page 97.

2 Practise with a partner. Talk about some things you do.

For example: A: *Most days I drink coffee in the morning. How about you?*
B: *Some days I drink coffee. But I drink tea three or four times a day!*

Describing schedules

1 Look at the table. It shows ways you can talk about schedules.

Preposition	Unit	Examples
on	day	on Monday, on Friday
at	time	at nine o'clock, at 8:30pm
in	month, year, part of day, season	in March, in 2010 in the morning, in spring
from … to …	day, time, month, year	from Monday to Thursday, from 4:00 to 6:00pm from April to June, from 2008 to 2010

2 Put the correct prepositions in the spaces. Check your answers with a partner.

a   The meeting starts _____ 10:00am.
b   _____ Monday _____ Wednesday I work in our head office.
c   _____ the afternoon I have a conference call with the US.
d   I take my holiday _____ August.
e   Lunchtime is _____ twelve-fifteen _____ one o'clock.
f   Men don't need to wear ties _____ summer.
g   I joined this company _____ 2007.
h   _____ Monday we have a morning meeting.

3   1.13   Listen and complete the schedule.

Hiro Makino: March Business Trip

___/3	12:05pm	Shanghai–New York (arrive _____.)
16/3	–	Inspect Factory Site
16/3		New York–Dallas
___/3	9:00am – 10:30pm	Texas Oil: Presentation
17/3		Dallas–SF
17/3	5:00pm –	SF Office: interview Lindsey Cole
17/3		Dinner: Dieter Muller (SF Manager)
18/3		SF–Shanghai (arrive 19/3 9:40pm)

4 Write true or false statements about Mr Makino's schedule.
Listen to your partner's statements. Are they true or false?

For example: *Mr Makino is arriving in Shanghai on 18th March.   False!*

a _____

b _____

c _____

Viewpoints Working hours

1 Read what these people say about working hours. Answer the questions.

- How many days a week do most people work in your country?
- Do most people work long hours in your country?
- How much holiday do people have in your country?

Maggie Kirk
Office Worker, Australia

I work for a busy property developer in Sydney. I travel a lot, so I'm a telecommuter. This means I can work from home, a hotel, or anywhere. I go to the office once or twice a month for meetings with my boss. I work a 40-hour week, but I can decide my schedule every day. This is good for me because I have two small children. I have four weeks' holiday every year, and I try to take time off in summer when my children are out of school.

Soo-hyun Park,
Administrative Staff, Korea

I start work at 8:30. I work five days a week for eight hours a day, with one hour off for lunch. When we are busy, I work overtime. Sometimes I work on Saturdays. In my first year with the company I had ten days off, but now I have 20 days a year. It's difficult for me to take more than four or five days at one time, because my job is very busy. Most people don't use all their holiday.

Michel Dubois,
Systems Engineer, France

In France, work-life balance is important. I work a 35-hour week from Monday to Friday. We have a flexitime system. I can decide when to come to the office, but I must be there between 10:00am and 3:00pm. In my company there is no overtime. We have five weeks' holiday every year. Many companies in France close for a month in the summer – my company closes for three weeks in August.

2 What is important to you when you look for a job?
Rate these items 1–5 (1 = very important, 5 = not important).

	Friendly colleagues	Flexitime	Interesting work	Long holidays	No overtime	Good salary	Telecommuting
Importance							

3 Talk about your answers in a group.

For example: A: *I think _____ is / are very important. How about you?*
B: *I don't think _____ is / are important. How about you?*

In business Describe your workday

Scenario: You are visiting your old high school as part of a 'careers day'. You and other people have been asked to talk to the students about a 'Typical Workday'.

1 Choose one of the following jobs (or use your own idea).

restaurant owner	high school teacher	construction worker	fashion designer
IT manager	ballet dancer	research scientist	Your own idea:

2 Complete the table with information about your workday.

Time	Place	Activity

3 Work in groups of three. Take turns describing your workday. When you listen to other group members, remember to react, reflect, and ask questions. Begin like this:

I'm a .... This is a typical workday. From / At .... I ...

I start work at 8:30 **UNIT 2**

UNIT 3

What does your company do?

Aims
- Giving information
- Asking about company background
- Asking for repetition and spelling
- Describing company business
- Viewpoints: What kind of company?
- In business: Describe your company

Listen and practise Giving information

1 Describe the photo. Where are the people? What are they talking about?

2 🔊 1.14 Andy is asking Eva about Euro Tech. Listen and circle the correct answer. Ask and answer the questions with a partner.

   a Was Euro Tech established in 1993?   Yes, it was.   No, it wasn't.
   b Is Euro Tech's head office in Paris?   Yes, it is.   No, it isn't.
   c Does Euro Tech have an office in Tokyo?   Yes, it does.   No, it doesn't.

3 🔊 1.14 Listen again and complete the conversation. Then practise with a partner. Take turns being Andy and Eva.

   Andy: Can I ask you some questions about Euro Tech?
   Eva: Yes, of course.
   Andy: _____ _____ _____ the company?
   Eva: We were established in 1992.
   Andy: I see. And _____ _____ _____ head office?
   Eva: In Munich. We also have offices in London and Paris.
   Andy: _____ _____ people work for Euro Tech?
   Eva: We have 45 full-time employees. 35 people work in our head office, and there are 10 workers in our other offices.

4 Practise the conversation again. Change the names and numbers in blue using the information below.

Company	Established	Employees	Head Office	Offices
Timson Watches	1835	150	Geneva (120)	London (10), New York (20)
Natural Beauty	1994	670	Milan (350)	New York (120), Hong Kong (200)
Tour Asia	2000	104	Singapore (60)	Beijing (20), Seoul (14), Bangkok (10)
Comet Technology	2003	19	Portland (10)	San Francisco (5), San Jose (4)

5 🔊 1.15 What do you think Andy will ask next? Tick (✓) your guesses. Then listen to see if you are correct.

a ☐ He will ask Eva where she lives. c ☐ He will ask Eva about her job.
b ☐ He will ask about Euro Tech's customers. d ☐ He will ask Eva for her telephone number.

Asking about company background

1 Look at the table. It shows questions you can ask about a company.

What		does	your company	do?
Where		is	your head office?	
When		was	the company	established?
How many	offices / employees	do	you	have?

2 🔊 1.16 Listen and complete the notes. Then check your answers with a partner.

a Batang Corp.
Established:
Head office: *Kuala Lumpur*
Offices:
Employees:
Business: *imports and exports goods*

b Insung Ltd.
Established:
Head office:
Offices:
Employees: *1,200*
Business: *supplies foodstuffs*

c BL Chemicals
Established:
Head office:
Offices: *80*
Employees:
Business: *produces plastic goods*

d Brown Construction
Established: *1913*
Head office:
Offices:
Employees:
Business: *designs and builds roads and bridges*

3   Look at the examples of long and short answers below.
    Then ask and answer the questions about the companies in exercise 2.

    When was _____ established?   It was established in (2003). / In (2003).
    How many employees does _____ have? It has (750) employees. / (750).
    Where is the head office of _____ ? The head office is in (Seoul). / In Seoul.
    How many offices does _____ have?   It has (four) offices. / (four).

4   Now ask and answer questions about Ruben Steel Corp. with a partner.

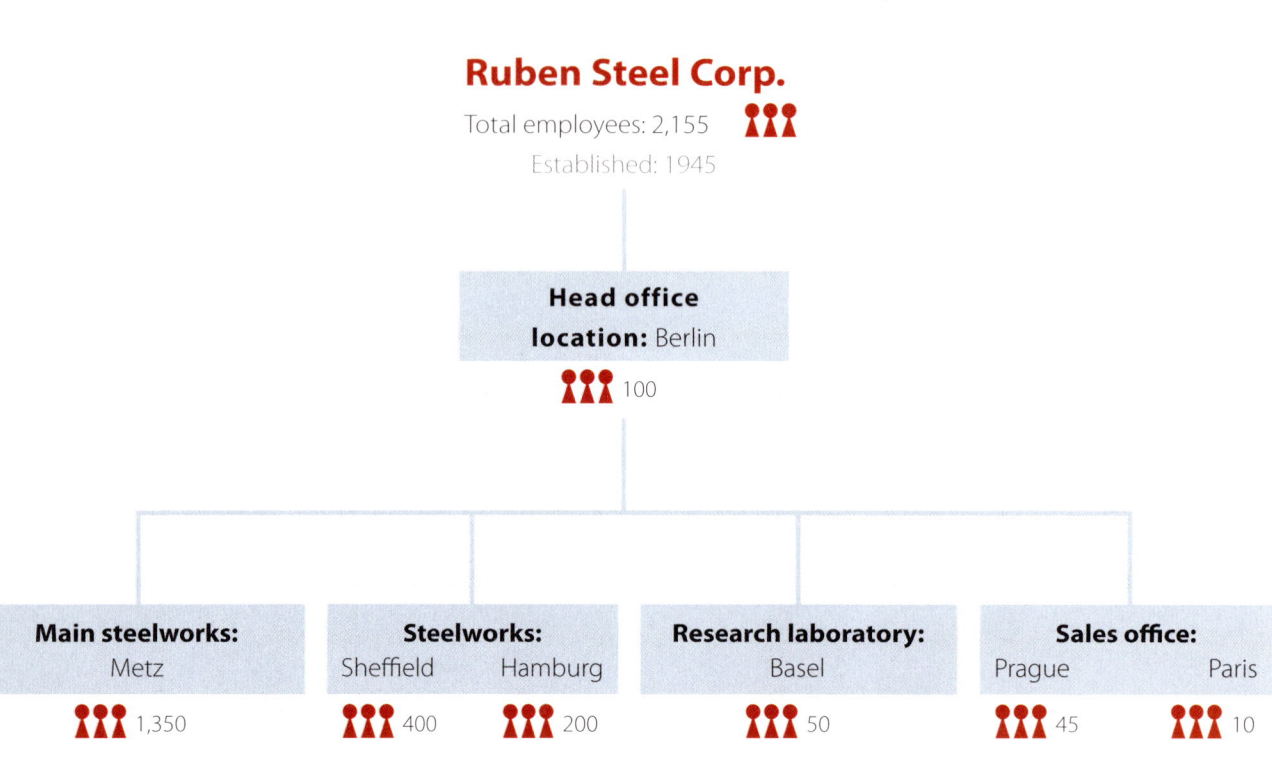

5   Practise with a partner. Student A, give an answer.
    Student B, ask the question.

    For example: A: *Two.*
                  B: *How many steelworks does Ruben Steel have?*

                  B: *In Berlin.*
                  A: *Where is the head office of Ruben Steel?*

Conversation strategy Asking for repetition and spelling

1   Look at the table. It shows ways you can ask someone
    to repeat or spell what he or she has said.

	can you repeat that?	
	can you say that again?	
	can you spell that?	
I'm sorry,		
	can you repeat / spell	your telephone number?
		the address?
		your family name?

Talk business

Student A, turn to page 86.

Student B, turn to page 98.

2   Practise with a partner. Take turns asking the questions.

Describing company business

Look at these ways you can talk about what companies do.

Euro Tech **designs** smart phones for the communications industry.

Web Talk **provides** translation of web pages.

1 🔊 1.17 Listen and draw a line from the company to the product. Then write the correct words from the box on the lines. You can use some words twice.

builds   develops   manufactures   sells   designs   produces

a   Brown Construction   *designs and builds*
b   Amazon   _____
c   BL Chemicals   _____
d   Rockstar   _____
e   Nisco   _____

books and CDs

video games

plastic goods

roads and bridges

integrated circuits

2 Complete the following sentences using companies you know. Talk about the companies with a partner.

a   _____ sells _____ .
b   _____ makes _____ .
c   _____ .
d   _____ .
e   _____ .

3 Ask and answer *yes / no* questions with a partner using the information in exercises 1 and 2.

Q: Does _____ sell _____ ?   A: Yes, it does. / No, it doesn't.
Q: Does _____ build _____ ?   A: Yes, it does. / No, it doesn't.

Viewpoints: What kind of company?

1 Answer these questions for yourself. Write T for true or F for false next to each sentence. Compare your answers with a partner.

   a   I want to work for a big company.
   b   I want to work in a foreign country.
   c   I want to stay at one company for a long time.

2 1.18 Listen to these people talk about their companies. Match the person with what they say.

- [ ] My company develops medicines.
- [ ] I work for a small family company.
- [ ] We have offices in New York, London and Tokyo.
- [ ] I like working for a big company.
- [ ] Everyone is friendly and I enjoy my job.
- [ ] I need to improve my English!

a Neil Parker,
Pharmacist, US

b George Weber,
Electrical Engineer, Germany

c Emiko Yamaguchi,
Banker, Japan

3 Look at these types of industries. Can you think of any more?

Raw materials	Manufacturing		Services	
Farming	Construction	IT & Software	Banking	Hospitality
Fishing	Electronics	Pharmaceuticals	Education	News media
Mining	the Automotive Industry		Entertainment	Tourism
	the Chemical Industry		Health care	Transportation

4 What kind of industry do you want to work in? Talk about the industries with a small group. Use some of these adjectives or other words you know.

   creative   difficult   exciting   interesting   challenging   well-paid

   For example: *I want to work in (the chemical industry) because it's interesting. How about you?*
   I want to work in (tourism) because I like to travel. How about you?

UNIT 3   Get Ready for International Business

In business | Describe your company

Scenario: Choose a business you know. A business-focused blog wants to interview someone in your company. Prepare an information sheet so that you are ready to answer questions about the company.

1 Complete the information sheet.

Company name and logo:

Company information:

Established:

Employees:

Head Office:

_____

_____

2 Write down the questions you would like to ask your partner about their company using the information sheet to help you.

_____
_____
_____
_____
_____
_____
_____
_____

3 Take it in turns to be the company representative and the interviewer. Use your information sheet to help you answer the questions. Begin like this:

May I ask you a few questions about your company?
Yes, of course.

UNIT 4 How do you like your job?

Aims
- Making small talk
- Talking about likes and dislikes
- Making suggestions
- Sounding polite
- Viewpoints: Corporate culture
- In business: Company survey

Listen and practise Making small talk

1 Describe the photo. Where are they? What are they doing?

2 1.19 Stefan is talking with Diane. Listen and tick (✓) whether she likes or dislikes these things.

		likes	dislikes
a	York	☐	☐
b	countryside	☐	☐
c	rain	☐	☐

3 1.19 Listen again and complete the conversation. Then practise with a partner. Take turns being Stefan and Diane.

Stefan: Hi, Diane. _____ do you _____ your new job here?
Diane: It's great. And I really like living in York. Although, it _____ rains a lot …
Stefan: It does, but that's why the countryside here is so _____.
Diane: That's true. I just _____ walking in the rain!

4 1.20 Diane talked about some things she didn't like. How will Stefan respond? Tick (✓) your guesses. Then listen to see if you are correct.

a ☐ He will agree with her.
b ☐ He will talk about something he doesn't like.
c ☐ He will suggest some things for her to buy.
d ☐ He will get angry.

Talking about likes and dislikes

1 To make small talk, people often share their likes and dislikes. Look at the table. It shows ways you can do this. Practise with a partner. Take turns reading the sentences.

	like	my job.
	enjoy	taking business trips.
I	don't mind	our cafeteria.
	don't like	queuing.
	can't stand	commuting.

2 Talk to your partner about some other activities that you like or dislike.

For example: A: *I like baseball. How about you?*
B: *Me too. I like baseball.*
Or
   Really? I can't stand baseball.

3 Look at the words in the box below. Are they positive or negative? Put them into the table. Then discuss your choices with a partner, and add some more words to each list.

attractive   boring   challenging   confusing   difficult
easy   exciting   frustrating   fun   interesting

positive
attractive

negative
boring

4 Look at ways you can give more information about likes and dislikes. Practise with a partner. Take turns being A and B.

A: How do you like your job?
   (question)

B: I love it. **It's great**.
   It's OK. **It's a little boring**.
   Actually, **it's frustrating**.

A: I like our new uniforms.
   (statement)

B: Yeah, me too. **They're attractive**.
   Really? Actually, **I can't stand them**!

5 Practise with a partner. Student A: read a question or statement. Student B: respond. Take turns asking and responding in different ways.

Questions	Statements
How do you like your new job?	I don't like long holidays.
How do you like living here?	I like working at the weekend.
How do you like the cafeteria food?	I like our new computers.
(your own idea)	(your own idea)

Making suggestions

1 🔊 1.21 When someone talks about something he or she doesn't like, you can make a suggestion. Listen to the sentences in the table. Then practise reading each sentence to a partner.

You should	ask your boss for a day off.
Why don't you	ask your boss for a day off?
I recommend	asking your boss for a day off.
How about	asking your boss for a day off?

2 🔊 1.22 Listen to four employees talking about their problems. What suggestion does someone make? Number them in order a–d as you hear them. There are two extra suggestions.

☐ I recommend taking an earlier train.
☐ Why don't you bring your own lunch?
☐ You should talk to your manager.
☐ Why don't you ask for more training?
☐ You should look for a new job.
☐ How about reading the manual?

Talk business

Student A, turn to page 87.

Student B, turn to page 99.

UNIT 4 Get Ready for International Business

3 Work in groups of three. Make suggestions for these situations. Spend five minutes on each situation. One person writes down the suggestions. Then share your ideas with the class.

- I need to get a birthday present for my dad, but I don't know what to get.
- I want to make some friends in other countries.
- I have a one-week holiday. I want to go somewhere interesting.

For example: *Why don't you go to Hawaii?*

Conversation strategy Sounding polite

Language can be polite or impolite, but your tone of voice – how you sound when you say something – is also very important.

1 Listen to these sentences said two different ways. The first way is polite; the second way is impolite.

Why don't you bring your own lunch?

You should talk to your manager.

2 Listen to the conversations. Pay attention to the speakers' tone of voice. Which responses sound polite? Which don't? Tick (✓) the appropriate box.

		polite	impolite
a	A: I don't know how to use this fax machine. B: It's really easy.	☐	☐
b	A: I feel exhausted! B: Why don't you sit down?	☐	☐
c	A: I don't have the company's phone number. B: How about looking it up online?	☐	☐
d	A: How can I get to the restaurant? B: How about taking a taxi?	☐	☐

3 Practise the conversations with a partner. Student B should first try to sound impolite. Practise again, and student B should try to sound polite. Take turns being A and B.

How do you like your job? **UNIT 4**

Viewpoints Corporate culture

1 Read what these employees from around the world say about the corporate culture in their companies.

Marcus Bodine, Software Designer, US

I work for a software company. We work hard, with a lot of overtime, but we have fun, too – for example, on Fridays, we wear casual clothes, like jeans and a Hawaiian shirt. Sometimes my group goes out for pizza together. And we always have a big company picnic in the summer. People bring their families, and we play softball.

Alma Hansson, Accounts Manager, Sweden

I started working last year for an IT company. It's easy for me to talk to my co-workers and my managers. My manager wants me to give my opinion. In Sweden, we don't talk about our families or hobbies at work. I don't usually talk about my job with my family. We don't mix our work lives and our personal lives.

Hassan Zouabi, Civil Servant, Egypt

I work in a government office in Cairo. I greet everyone in my office each day. Respect, good manners, and relationships between people are important! I talk and socialise with my co-workers while I work. Our managers praise the workers often. This makes us want to work harder.

2 Discuss these questions with a group.

- Which company or companies seem similar to ones in your country? Which are different?
- Which work customs do you think you'd like? Are there any you wouldn't like?
- Imagine you work for a company that you like very much. Tell your group three things that make it a good company to work for.

In business | Company survey

Scenario: You work for a global manufacturing company. Your group has been asked to do a survey to find out how satisfied people are with their working conditions. Interview other members of the class about what they like and don't like.

1. Complete the table with notes on your own likes and dislikes. Remember to say why you like or dislike something.

	Likes (why?)	Dislikes (why?)
Overseas Business Trips		
Meetings		
Presentations		
Writing Reports		
Visiting Customers		
Your own:		

2. Work in pairs or groups of three. Ask and answer questions about each other's likes and dislikes. For example:

   Do you like going on overseas business trips?
   Yes, I do. It's exciting to visit new places. / No, I don't. It's hard for me to speak English all the time.
   Do you like visiting customers?
   Yes, I do. I like meeting new people. / No, I don't. I get nervous.

3. With a different pair or group, talk about your likes and dislikes. Choose two areas and complete the following word webs with information you have collected.

   LIKES   **DISLIKES**

   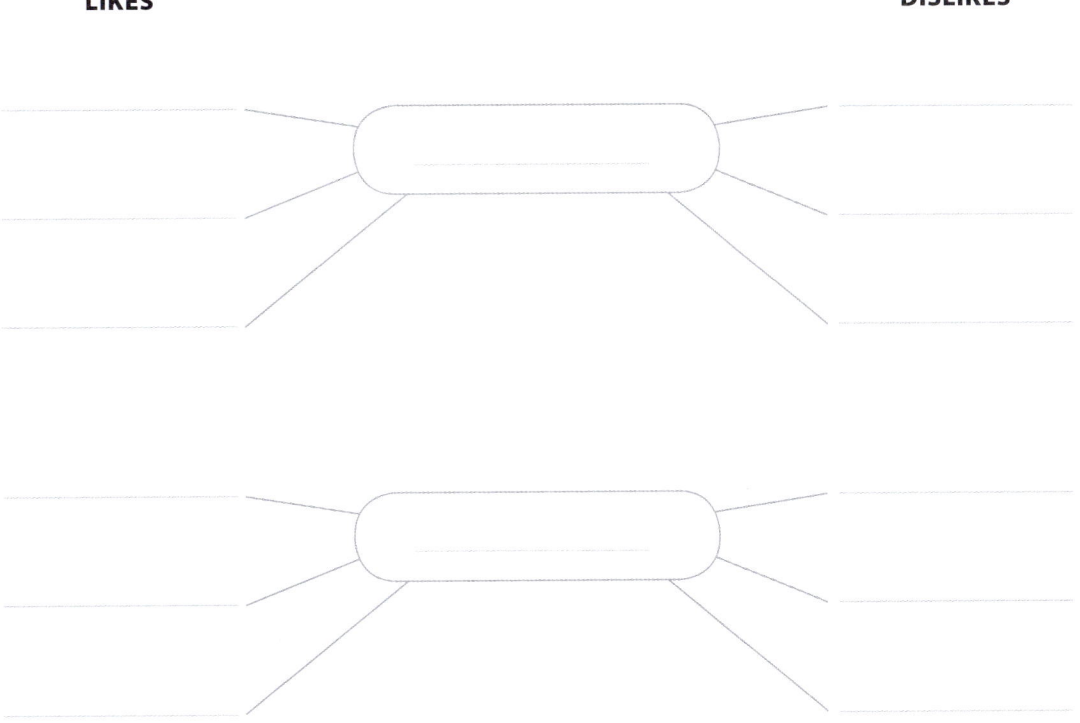

4. Share your word webs with other class members.

How do you like your job? **UNIT 4**

Review: Units 1–4

1 Sentence scramble

Unscramble the sentences. Then number them in the correct order to make a conversation. Then practise with a partner.

interesting wow Bangkok that's ! _____ !
office head in our Bangkok is . _____ .
company old is how the ?   1 _____ ?
where head office your is ? _____ ?
1956 were established we in . _____ .

2 Face-to-face

Use these cards to introduce yourself to a partner.

Timson Watches
Geneva, London, New York

Ben Poole
Product Planner
Tel: 7858-465-9979
Email: poole-b@timsonwatches.com

Ruhr Pipe Mfg.

MIKEL DEUTER   Service Engineer
Mikel_Deuter@ruhrpipe.co.de   051-726-7853

Start the conversation.
↓
Introduce yourself.
↓
Talk about your job (exchange cards).
↓
End the conversation.

3 Crossword

Look at the clues and complete the puzzle.

Across:
1 I can't do this puzzle. It's too d_____
3 I need to learn many new things in my job. It's c_____ but I enjoy it.
5 I don't mind studying English. Sometimes it's i_____
6 I can't stand housework. It's so b_____

Down:
2 I like this puzzle a lot. It's f_____
4 I enjoy visiting new places. It's e_____

4 Matching pairs

Connect A and B to make questions.

1	Can you	a	do you work for?
2	Where	b	Nissan build cars?
3	Why don't	c	was Amazon established?
4	How do you	d	about you?
5	Who	e	repeat that?
6	How	f	do you do?
7	When	g	offices do you have?
8	How about	h	you study harder?
9	Does	i	like your job?
10	How many	j	do you work?
11	What	k	taking a rest?

5 Happy and sad

 1.25

Listen to these five people. React (e.g. 'Wow!', 'Really?', 'I'm sorry to hear that') when you hear the beep.

6 Daily life

Complete the information for yourself. Describe your routine to a partner. When you listen, remember to reflect / react.

	wake up at _____ .
	eat _____ for breakfast.
Every day	
Most days	I _____ .
Some days	
	_____ .
	go to sleep at _____ .

7 Which preposition?

Put the correct prepositions in the spaces.

I met my friend _____ 12 o'clock _____ Saturday. _____ 12:30 _____ three we went bowling. _____ the evening we went to karaoke. Next week _____ the 14th we are going hiking. _____ summer we are going on holiday to the USA together.

8 Company profile

Ask and answer questions about Natural Beauty with a partner. Then give an answer and ask someone to make the question.

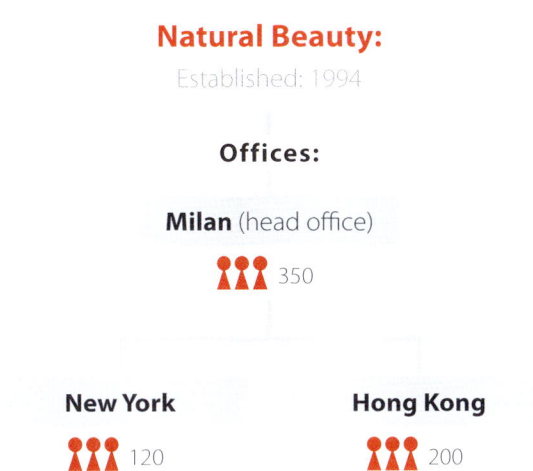

Natural Beauty:
Established: 1994

Offices:

Milan (head office)
350

New York   **Hong Kong**
120   200

9 What's the matter?

1.26 Jill has many problems. Listen and make a suggestion when you hear the beep. You can use the ideas here or make your own. Remember to sound polite!

go to the bank
drink some water
take a rest
take some medicine
eat lunch
call the help desk

UNIT 5

Can I take a message?

Aims
- Talking on the phone
- Answering the phone
- Controlling language
- Taking a message
- Ending a call
- Viewpoints: Mobile phones
- In business: Receiving and passing on messages

Listen and practise Talking on the phone

1 Describe the photos. Where are they? What are they saying?

2 🔊 1.27 Listen to the telephone call. Write T for true or F for false next to each sentence. Then check your answers with a partner.

a Sam wants to speak to Vincent. _____   b Vincent is out of the office. _____

3 🔊 1.27 Listen again and complete the conversation. Then practise with a partner. Take turns being the receptionist and Sam.

Receptionist: Prima Donna Fashions. How can I help you?
Sam: Hello, can I _____ _____ Vincent Campbell please?
Receptionist: Can I have _____ _____ please?
Sam: It's Sam Montpellier from Fierce Fabrics.
Receptionist: I'm sorry, I can't hear you. Can you repeat that?
Sam: Yes, of course. It's Sam Montpellier from Fierce Fabrics.
Receptionist: Thank you, Mr Montpellier. I'll transfer your call.
Vincent: Hello, _____ _____ Vincent _____.

4 Practise the conversation again. Change the names in blue using the information below.

Caller	Receptionist	Receiver
Mary Chan (Pacific Finance)	Tour Asia	Lek Phikul
Jeff Howes (C&F Stores)	Timson Watches	Ben Poole
Mike Burns (Golden Palace)	Snappy Snack Foods	Nancy Chen

5 🔊 1.28 What do you think Sam will say next? Tick (✓) your guesses. Then listen to see if you are correct.

a ☐ How are you?
b ☐ Vincent, can I meet you today?
c ☐ Vincent, this is Sam Montpellier. How are you?
d ☐ I'm calling to ask if we can meet today.

Answering the phone

1 Look at the table. It shows ways you can answer the phone.

	morning.		Can I help you?
Good	afternoon.	(Comet Technologies).	How can I help you?
	evening.		May I help you?

2 🔊 1.29 Listen and repeat what you hear. Use the same intonation.

a Good morning. Northwest Media Services … ?
b Good evening. Corporate Training Solutions … ?
c Good afternoon. Aztec Coffee … ?
d Good morning. Marco Supermarkets … ?

Conversation strategy Controlling language

1 Write the questions (a–e) next to the correct category to show different ways of controlling language. Check your answers with a partner.

a Can you speak more loudly?
b Can you repeat that?
c How do you spell (that)?
d Can you speak more slowly?
e Can you say that again?

Speed _____   _____ Volume

Controlling language

Repetition _Can you repeat that?_   _____ Spelling

(**Note:** English speakers sometimes say *Speak louder* in informal situations.)

2 🔊 1.30 Listen to four conversations and write the letter (a–d) of the question you hear.

a _____ b _____ c _____ d _____

Taking a message

1 🔊 1.31 Listen to the conversation. Then practise with a partner.

Receptionist: Ashwell Transportation. How can I help you?

Caller: Can I speak to Kevin Aston, please? This is Tim Horowitz.

Receptionist: Just a moment, please. … Hello? I'm sorry, but Mr Aston is in a meeting. Can I take a message?

2 Practise the conversation with a different partner. Change the information in blue using your real names and the information below.

out of the office	on holiday	not at his desk
on a business trip	off sick	on another line

3 Look at the table. It shows phrases you can use for messages.

	Yes.	Please ask her to call me back.
		Please tell her I called.
Can I take a message?		
	No,	thank you. I'll call back later.
		that's OK. Thank you.

4 Practise with a partner. Use this conversation map.

Caller:

'Ring, ring.'

Ask to speak to Ms …

Repeat slowly.

Give name.

Give name again.

Respond.

Receptionist:

Give company name.

Ask caller to repeat that. Ask caller to speak more slowly.

Ask for caller's name.

Ask caller to speak louder.

Ask caller to wait. Tell caller that Ms / Mr … is (*not there*). Offer to take a message.

34 UNIT 5 Get Ready for International Business

5 Listen and complete the messages below.

a

2:40
Tom,
Margaret _____ from _____ Corporation called. Can you call her back after _____?
Her number is 090 - _____ - _____.
Hisako.

b

Josh Brown

Date: 22nd March   Time: 09:30

Message: José _____ from the Philippines called.
He will call you back _____.

Taken by: Maria

c

Caller: Manuel _____ of Aztec Coffee

Tel:

Message:

Received by: Heena   Time: 10:25

d

From: Alison Chen
To: Peter Weybridge
Subject: <Important> Telephone Call

Peter,

Ms. _____ from _____ called this morning.
Can you call her back as soon as possible?

Her number is 01 _____ 87 _____.

Regards,
Alison

Ending a call

1 Look at these ways of ending a phone call.

Receiver	Caller
a I'll give (her) your message.	
b Thank you for calling.	e Thank you.
c Thank you for your call.	f Goodbye.
d Goodbye.	

2 Listen again to the conversations in exercise 5. Which phrases do they use to end the calls? Write the letters in the boxes for each conversation.

a ☐☐☐☐   c ☐☐☐☐
b ☐☐☐☐   d ☐☐☐☐

Talk business

Student A, turn to page 88.

Student B, turn to page 100.

Can I take a message? **UNIT 5** **35**

Viewpoints Mobile phones

1 Answer these questions for yourself. Compare your answers with other class members.
   - Do you have a mobile phone?
   - What do people in your country use mobile phones for?

2 1.33 Listen to people from three different countries talking about their mobile phones. Tick (✓) the sentences you hear.

Hye-won Park, Sales Clerk, Korea

- I send 20 to 30 text messages a day.
- I don't use it at the office.
- I can use my phone as a train pass.
- It's not convenient.

Melissa Golding, Student, US

- ☐ My parents call me every week.
- ☐ I don't text much – it's easier and cheaper to email.
- ☐ I feel safe if I'm driving.
- ☐ I hate it when people use their phones in restaurants.

Thomas Müeller, Engineer, Germany

- The company uses it to contact me.
- I like to play games.
- I also read the news on the internet.
- I use the alarm when I stay in hotels.

3 Discuss these questions in a small group.
   - Which person is most like you (or people from your country)?
   - Are there any rules in your country about where you cannot use mobile phones?
   - Do people in your country use mobile phones on buses and trains? In restaurants?

4 What functions are important to you when you buy or use a mobile phone? Rate these items 1–5 (1 = very important, 5 = not important). Talk about your answers in a group.

Colour		Camera		Music	
Size		Internet		Games	
Cost		TV		Text messages	
Alarm		Calculator		Schedule	
(Your idea)					

36 UNIT 5 Get Ready for International Business

In business — Receiving and passing on messages

Scenario: You work in a sales office with two colleagues. Both of your colleagues are away from the office. You will need to take messages for them while they are away. You also need to call two customers. If the customers are not there, leave a message.

1. In the space below, write down your name, your company name, and your telephone number.

   Name:

   Company Name:

   Tel:

2. On a piece of paper, write down the names of your two colleagues so the rest of your class can see them.

3. Work in groups of four. With different partners, make and receive two phone calls. Use the forms below to write down the messages you receive.

Message for:	Message for:
Caller:	Caller:
Company:	Company:
Tel:	Tel:

   ☐ Please call back
   ☐ Will call you back
   ☐ No message
   ☐ Other

   ☐ Please call back
   ☐ Will call you back
   ☐ No message
   ☐ Other

   Message:

   Message:

   Received by: Time:

   Received by: Time:

4. After you have made and received your calls, check with your partners that the information in the messages is correct.

Can I take a message? **UNIT 5** 37

UNIT 6 Which ones should we order?

Aims
- Discussing products
- Describing and comparing products
- Understanding advertisements
- Softening language
- Viewpoints: Advertising
- In business: Advertise your company

COSTA DEL COOL

Trip Tees

material: _____ % cotton
_____ % polyester
country: Spain
No. of colours: _____

material: _____ % bamboo
_____ % cotton
country: _____
No. of colours: _____

Listen and practise Discussing products

1 Describe the photos. What do they show?

2 🔊 1.34 Juan is giving a presentation to the Purchasing Department. Listen and tick (✓) which T-shirts he prefers.
  ☐ Costa del Cool
  ☐ Trip Tees

3 🔊 1.34 Listen again and complete the brochures with the correct information. Check your answers with a partner.

4 🔊 1.35 How else will Juan compare the two companies? What will he talk about? Tick (✓) your guesses. Then listen to see if you are correct.
  a ☐ price   b ☐ size   c ☐ quality   d ☐ style

Describing and comparing products

1 Look at the table. It shows words you can use to describe products. Complete the table with a partner. Can you think of any more words?

	-er / -ier	more - (than)
cheap	cheaper	
compact		more compact
easy	easier	
energy-efficient		
fast		
heavy		
light		
new		
reliable		

2 Look at the table again and talk with a partner. When do you add *-er* to a word? *-ier*? When do you use *more*? Note these exceptions:

good - better
bad - worse
fun - more fun

3 Read the conversation with a partner.

A: This looks like a great camera. And it's really cheap.
B: Yeah. But I think that one is cheaper. It's also more compact.
A: Hmm. You're right. That's important.

4 Practise the conversation again. Change the products and the descriptions in blue using the ideas below.

a **camera**
light; compact

b **software package**
fast; new

c **mobile phone**
energy-efficient; easy to use

d **video game**
fun; challenging

e **jacket**
attractive; cheap

f **shredder**
compact; reliable

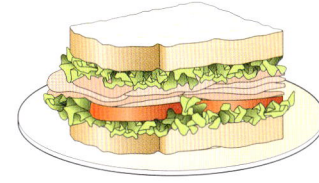

g **sandwich**
cheap; delicious

h **scooter**
reliable; energy-efficient

Understanding advertisements

1 Match the words and phrases with their definitions.

a buy one, get one free __3__
b coupon _____
c a 10% discount; 10% off _____
d free shipping _____
e money-back guarantee _____
f on sale _____

1 When you order something, you only pay for the item. You don't pay any mailing costs.
2 A product costs 10% less than it usually does.
3 If you buy one product, you get another one without paying any more money.
4 If you don't like the product, you can return it and the shop will return your money.
5 A product costs less money than it usually does.
6 A piece of paper that promises you can pay less money or get some money back (a refund).

2 1.36 Listen and complete the advertisements.

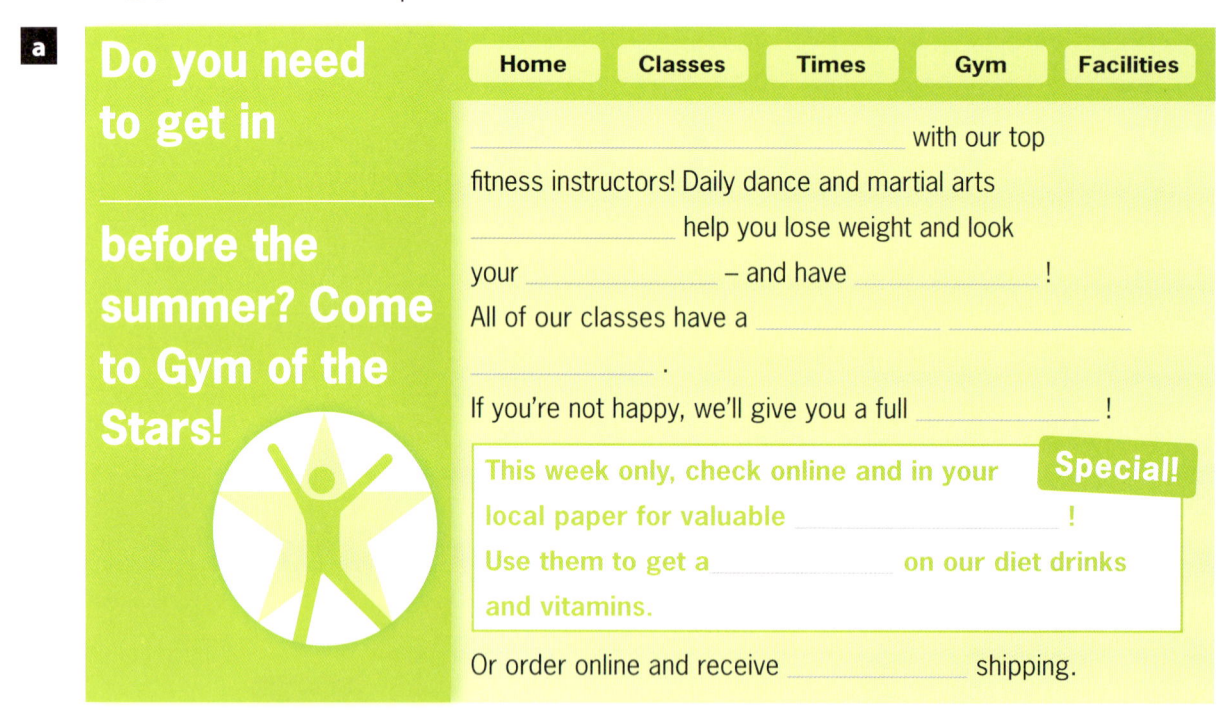

a

Do you need to get in _____ before the summer? Come to Gym of the Stars!

| Home | Classes | Times | Gym | Facilities |

_____ with our top fitness instructors! Daily dance and martial arts _____ help you lose weight and look your _____ – and have _____!
All of our classes have a _____ _____ _____.
If you're not happy, we'll give you a full _____!

Special! This week only, check online and in your local paper for valuable _____!
Use them to get a _____ on our diet drinks and vitamins.

Or order online and receive _____ shipping.

b

Total Fitness

When you're _____ about your health, you're ready for Total Fitness!

Work with a fitness instructor to get _____ results. You'll look and _____ better.

Sign up with a friend, and you'll each get _____ off the first month's fee.

Pay for a one-year membership and get _____!

Talk business
Student A, turn to page 89.
Student B, turn to page 101.

UNIT 6 Get Ready for International Business

Conversation strategy Softening language

1 Listen to the two conversations between a Sales Assistant and a customer. Which one is more polite? Why?

Conversation 1
A: How do you like this printer?
B: Well, it's kind of large, don't you think?
A: Hmmm. But it's easy to use.
B: I don't know. It's also not very energy-efficient.

Conversation 2
A: How do you like this watch?
B: It's too small.
A: Hmmm. But it's attractive.
B: It's also not cheap.

2 Practise Conversation 1 with a partner. Underline the phrases in the first conversation that soften the expression, to make it less direct. Add those phrases to Conversation 2. Then practise with a partner.

3 Look at the table. It shows ways that you can soften your language.

Instead of *too*	Instead of *not*	At the beginning of a sentence		At the end of a sentence
a bit	not very	Well…	To be honest…	…don't you think?
kind of	not really	Actually…	I don't know.	
rather	not so			

4 Listen to these conversations comparing products. Write down the softening language they use.

a

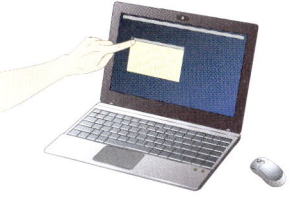

b

5 Talk about these products with a partner.

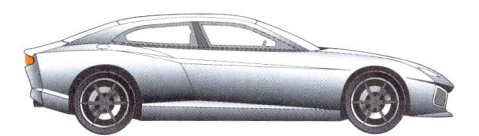

expensive, fast, energy-efficient

small, cheap, difficult-to-use

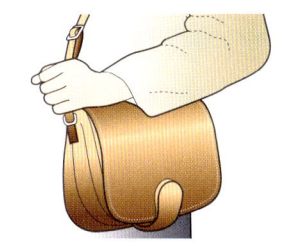

expensive, fashionable, practical

heavy, compact, expensive

Viewpoints Advertising

1 Read what these people from around the world say about advertisements.

Helen Curtis,
Nurse, UK

I'm annoyed by most ads. I don't like ads interrupting radio or TV programmes. That's why I mostly watch the BBC, which doesn't have any ads. These days, magazines seem to be mostly ads! Even some articles are really just trying to sell you a product. I'm especially annoyed by internet ads. When I'm trying to read a website, I don't like large flashing ads for some product I'm not interested in.

Ayako Awano,
Designer, Japan

Actually, I like a lot of TV ads. In Japan, companies never compare themselves directly to another company or criticise their competitors. So the ads focus on giving you a good impression of the product and the company. Many ads on TV today are funny or clever. They use a lot of attractive images, popular music, and celebrities. In fact, sometimes the ads are better than the programmes!

Henri Latour,
Student, France

I don't pay much attention to TV ads, so they don't bother me. I'm not impressed by celebrity endorsements, though – I don't believe a car is better because someone famous drives it. I look at internet ads sometimes. It's a good way to find special offers, coupons, and discounts. I don't mind ads if they save me money.

2 Discuss these questions in a group.

- Which person is most like you?
- What kinds of ads annoy you? What kinds of ads do you like?
- How often do you see ads? Where do you see them?
- What do you think about celebrity endorsements? What famous people advertise products that you know about? Have you ever bought any of those products?

In business: Advertise your company

Scenario: Your group have been asked to create some advertising for a company. Create an advert that will encourage people to buy their products or use their services.

1 Discuss in your group. Make notes.

- What product or service you are advertising. What is it called?
- Where the advert is going to appear (TV, magazine, radio, web, etc.)
- What words you are going to use to describe the product or service.
- If you are going to include any special offers (discounts, coupons, etc.)
- If you are going to use other ideas (celebrity endorsements, comparisons with other products, surveys, etc.)

2 Write a slogan for your product or service. A slogan is a short sentence or phrase that helps a product or service to sell.

Think of some examples of products and their slogans that you know in your group.

Write your own slogan for your product as a group.

3 Plan the advert here. Either write the script, or design the advert.

4 Describe your ideas to the class.

UNIT 7
Are you free on Tuesday?

Aims
- Making arrangements
- Making a telephone call
- Checking information
- Making an appointment
- Viewpoints: Using technology to communicate
- In business: Make an appointment

Listen and practise Making arrangements

1 Describe the photos. Where are they? What are they doing?

2 1.39 Listen to the telephone call. Write T for true or F for false next to each sentence. Then check your answers with a partner.

   a   Carolyn wants to meet Amanda next week. _____
   b   Amanda is busy on Tuesday afternoon. _____

3 1.39 Listen again and complete the conversation. Then practise with a partner. Take turns being Carolyn and Amanda.

Carolyn: Hi Amanda, this is Carolyn. How are you?
Amanda: Hi Carolyn! I'm fine, thanks. How are you?
Carolyn: Very well, thank you. _____ _____ _____ ask if we can meet this week.
Amanda: Certainly. _____ _____ _____ my diary. When is good for you?
Carolyn: _____ _____ _____ on Tuesday at ten?
Amanda: Let me see. No, sorry. _____ _____ _____. I'm free in the afternoon. How about half past two?
Carolyn: Half past two is fine.

4 Practise the conversation again. Change the information in blue using your real names and the times below.

Caller	Receiver	
on Wednesday at three	in the morning	eleven
on the 25th	on the 26th	four o'clock
tomorrow at nine	on Tuesday	half past nine
Friday evening	in the afternoon	half past three

44   UNIT 7   Get Ready for International Business

5 1.40 What do you think Carolyn will say next? Tick (✓) your guesses. Then listen to see if you are correct.

a ☐ She will ask where they will meet.
b ☐ She will repeat the day and time.
c ☐ She will tell Amanda why she wants to meet.
d ☐ She will ask Amanda for her email address.

Making a telephone call

1 Look at the table. It shows ways you can begin a telephone call.

	Can I speak to	Mr / Ms .... , please? the Sales Manager, please? room service, please?
Hello, … Hello, this is … Hello, my name is …	I'm calling to I'd like to	change (my reservation). confirm (our meeting time). order (some flowers).
	I'm calling about	(our meeting tomorrow). (your email). (my reservation).
	I'm returning your call.	

2 1.41 Listen and connect the receiver with the caller and the purpose / subject.

Receiver	Caller	Purpose / Subject
a Toni's Pizza	Mario Fera	Make a reservation
b Jaidev Singh	Junji Tanaka	Meeting time
c Westwood Hotel	Josh Brown	Order food
d José Reina	Rachel Carson	Returning a call

3 Practise making calls with a partner using the information below. Take turns being the receiver and the caller.

Receiver	Caller
a Grand Hotel Receptionist	Call the Grand Hotel to change your reservation.
b Bill Smith	Call Bill Smith to change your meeting time.
c Maria Vega	Call Maria Vega to return her call.
d Sunset Holidays	Call Sunset Holidays to confirm your reservation.

Conversation strategy Checking information

1 Look at the table. It shows ways you can check information or confirm that you understand what someone has said.

Let me confirm.	Your number is …	
Let me repeat that.	You said …	Is that right?
	You want to change …	
	Thursday at six o'clock.	

2 1.42 Listen to the call. Follow this conversation map.

Caller:	Receptionist:
'Ring, ring.'	Give the company name. Offer to help.
Ask to speak to …	Ask for the caller's name.
Give your name.	Ask the caller to spell his / her family name.
Spell your family name.	
	Ask the caller to wait. Tell the caller that Ms / Mr … is (*out of the office*). Offer to take a message.
Ask him / her to call you back.	
Give the telephone number.	Ask the caller for their telephone number.
	Ask the caller to speak more slowly.
Repeat the telephone number.	Check the information (*telephone number*).
Agree.	Check the information (*name, number, message*).
Agree.	End the call.
End the call.	

3 Practise with a partner using the conversation map in exercise 2. Use your own ideas for company, names, number, and message. Use the chart to make notes.

Company: _____
Name: _____
Number: _____
Message: _____

Talk business
Student A, turn to page 90.
Student B, turn to page 102.

Making an appointment

1 Look at the tables. They show phrases you can use to make appointments.

| When are you free?
When is good for you?
What time is good for you? | → | I'm free | (on Tuesday).
(at 11:30). |

| Are you free | (on Monday)?
(at two o'clock)?
(on the 25th)? | → | Sorry,
Yes, | I'm busy then.
I'm free then. |

| How about | (Monday)?
(five o'clock)? | → | That's fine.
Five o'clock is fine. |

2 🎧 1.43 Listen to these conversations. Where and when will they meet? Check your answers with a partner.

Conversation 1

Day:

Time:

Place:

Conversation 2

Day:

Time:

Place:

Conversation 3

Day:

Time:

Place:

3 Practise with a partner using your own names. Follow this conversation map.

Caller:

'Ring, ring.'

Give your name.
Ask how he / she is.

Reply. Say you are calling to ask if he / she is free for a meeting.

Ask if he / she is free on (day).

Say that is fine. Ask if he / she is free at (time).

Confirm day and time.

End the call.

Receiver:

Give your name.
Offer to help.

Reply and reflect (*And you?*).

Say you will check your schedule.
Ask when is good for him / her.

Say you are busy then.
Give another day.

Agree.

Agree.

End the call.

Are you free on Tuesday? **UNIT 7** **47**

Viewpoints: Using technology to communicate

1. 🔊 1.44 Listen to people from three different countries talking about how they communicate. Make notes as you listen.

Silvia Rossi, Project Manager, Italy

Email:
Voicemail:
Telephone:
Teleconference:
Meetings:

Tran Chung Nguyen, Assistant Sales Manager, Vietnam

Email:
Voicemail:
Telephone:
Teleconference:
Meetings:

Masako Mori, HR Officer, Japan

Email:
Voicemail:
Telephone:
Teleconference:
Meetings:

2. Tick (✓) the boxes with your own information.

	Use	Don't use	Like	Don't like
Email				
Telephone				
Teleconference				
Face-to-face				
Text messages				
Chat				

3. Talk about your answers in a small group. Use some of this vocabulary.

complicated   efficient   formal   inefficient   informal   quick   simple   slow

For example:
A: *Do you use email?*
B: *Yes, I do. / No, I don't. How about you?*
A: *I like email because it's quick. What do you think?*
C: *Me too. I don't like chat because it's informal. How about you?*

UNIT 7 Get Ready for International Business

In business | Make an appointment

Scenario: You are new to a company and want to arrange short meetings with people from other departments in the company. You must arrange at least six meetings.

1. Complete the schedule with at least three or four things you have to do this week (meetings, business trips, studying, lunch appointments, etc.) and schedule times for them.

	MONDAY	TUESDAY	WEDNESDAY	THURSDAY	FRIDAY
9:00		Visit			
10:00		Customer			
11:00				Meeting	
12:00	Lunch			Lunch	
1:00					
2:00					
3:00					
4:00					
5:00					
6:00			Teleconference		

2. Work with a partner, make a phone call and decide on a time to meet that is convenient for you both and write down their name and their department in the correct place.

3. Change partners and make a new phone call until you have at least six appointments made with members of your class.

Are you free on Tuesday? **UNIT 7**

UNIT 8

Where's the Marketing Department?

Aims

- Getting directions
- Prepositions of place
- Giving a tour
- Viewpoints: Workplace facilities
- In business: Give a company tour

Listen and practise Getting directions

1 Describe the photos. Where are they? What are they saying?

2 🔊 1.45 Listen to the conversation. Circle the correct answer.

a Brett is at *his / someone else's* company.

b Brett *knows / doesn't know* where to go.

3 🔊 1.45 Listen again and complete the conversation. Then practise with a partner. Take turns being the receptionist and Brett.

Receptionist: Can I _____ you?

Brett: Yes. I'm Brett Silvermann, and I have a 3:00 appointment with Jack McAvoy in Marketing.

Receptionist: OK, Mr Silvermann, you can go _____ up.

Brett: Thanks. Uh… how do I _____ _____ the Marketing Department?

Receptionist: Oh, it's on the third floor. When you _____ out of the lift, turn right and _____ _____ the hall. It's the second door on your left, and it says "Marketing Department" on it. You can't _____ it.

Brett: Thanks. Oh, and, uh, _____ the lift?

4 Practise the conversation again. Change the information in blue using the times and places below.

Brett	10:30am meeting	Production
	lunch appointment	Sales
	2:00pm appointment	Accounting

Receptionist	seventh	turn right	the first room after the stairs	Production
	second	go straight	the last room on your right	Sales
	fourth	turn left	just after the drinking fountain	Accounting

5 🔊 1.46 What do you think the receptionist will do next? Tick (✓) your guesses. Then listen to see if you are correct.

a ☐ She will tell Brett where the lift is.   c ☐ She will call Mr McAvoy in Marketing.
b ☐ She will draw a map.   d ☐ She will take Brett to the third floor.

Prepositions of place

1 Where is the desk? Label each picture with words and phrases from the box.

across from   between   in the corner   next to / on the right
behind   in front of   next to / on the left   under

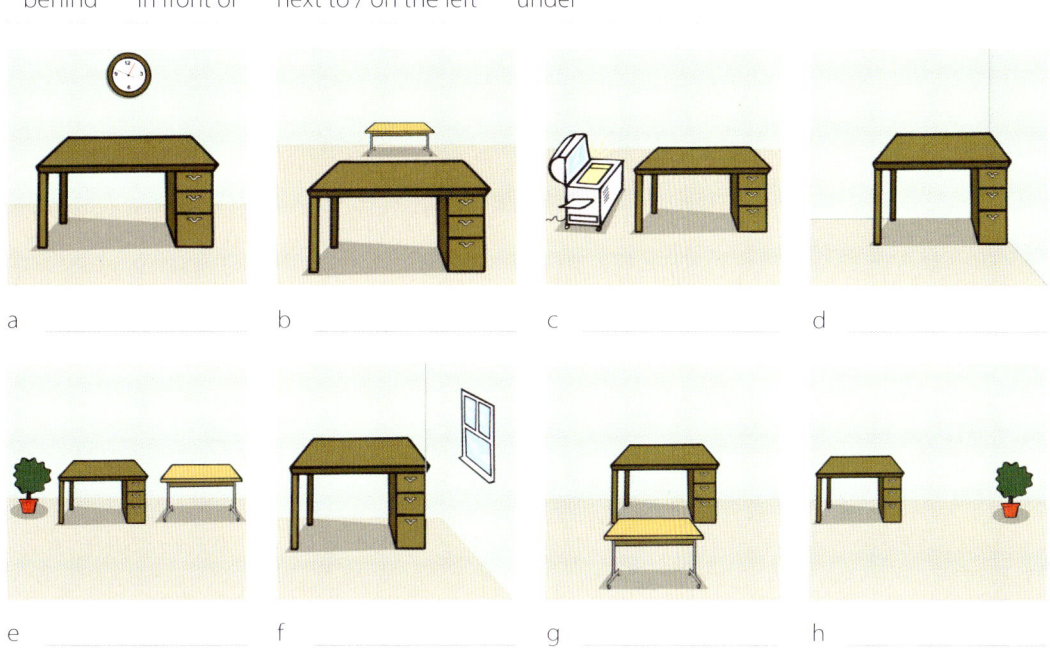

a _____   b _____   c _____   d _____

e _____   f _____   g _____   h _____

2 🔊 1.47 Listen to two people talking about an office. Label the desks that belong to these people. Write the correct letter on the desk.

a the boss   b the personal assistant   c Ken   d Sophie

Where's the Marketing Department? **UNIT 8**

3 Look at the office on page 51. Practise with a partner asking and answering questions about the picture.

For example: A: *Excuse me. Where's the fax machine?*
  B: *Oh, it's over there, next to Sophie's desk, on the right.*

Now ask and answer questions about these things:

a coffee maker   b plant   c water cooler   d exit

Giving a tour

1 1.48 Listen to a hotel manager showing the hotel to a new front desk receptionist. Practise the conversation with a partner. Take turns being the manager and the receptionist.

Manager:	Come with me, please. OK, this is the lobby, of course. There's a cash machine in the corner there. Oh, and a public phone, next to the cash machine. Any questions?
Receptionist:	Yes, is the lobby open 24 hours?
Manager:	Yes, it is. Now, let's go to the lifts. They're next to the stairs. This lift on the left goes only to the rooms. It doesn't stop on the first, second, or third floors. And this one here, this one stops on every floor. We'll go to the first floor to begin – that's the dining room and the lounge – and then to the second floor, the business centre. Um, any questions so far?
Receptionist:	What's on the third floor?
Manager:	The swimming pool and the fitness centre. OK, come with me.

2 Look at the table. It shows directions and questions you can use when you talk to groups of people.

Directions	Questions
Come with me, please.	Any questions?
Follow me.	Is that clear?
	Are you with me so far?
Listen carefully.	
Watch closely.	Can everyone hear me?
	Can everyone see?
Let's go now.	
Let's stop here.	Is everyone with me?

Talk business

Student A, turn to page 91.

Student B, turn to page 103.

3 Listen to these group tours. Tick (✓) the question that you hear. Then write the response.

a ☐ Are you with me so far?
  ☐ Is everyone with me?   *No, Sandy's at the drinking fountain.*

b ☐ Can everyone see?
  ☐ Any questions?   _____

c ☐ OK? Is that clear?
  ☐ OK? Can you hear?   _____

d ☐ Is everyone here?
  ☐ Can everyone hear me?   _____

4 Work in groups of 3–5. One of you is the HR Manager of a factory. The others are new employees. Take turns being the manager and give the new employees a tour. Use the map below. Start at the "X."

Begin like this:

OK, follow me, please. Let's go straight down this path. On the left is the research laboratory. …

Where's the Marketing Department? **UNIT 8**

Viewpoints Workplace facilities

1 Read what these people say about their workplaces.

Rodrigo de Santos,
Marketing Executive, Brazil

I work for a small marketing company. At the office, we only have a small cafeteria and some vending machines. But my company gives us discounts at many local businesses, including restaurants, shops, health clinics, hotels, and a health club.

Young-kwang Oh,
Factory Worker, Korea

I work in a factory. Because we often work overtime, and because there are a lot of different shifts, workers don't always have time to go shopping during the week. So we have a small convenience store on site, and also a cash machine, a chemist, a hairdresser's, and a laundry service.

Lise Martin,
Clerk, Canada

I work for an insurance company. Ten years ago, we had on-site daycare. But the company found out that working parents preferred a flexible schedule. Now we have facilities like a cafeteria, a gym, and a locker room. There's also a yoga class that meets twice a week during the lunch hour.

2 Imagine you are working at a medium-sized company five years from now. How important would these facilities be to you? Tick (✓) the appropriate column.

	Very important / necessary	Not necessary, but attractive	Not interesting or useful to me
on-site daycare			
a gym			
a cafeteria			
a convenience store			
a bank or a cash machine			
a chemist			
a hairdresser's			
showers			
a travel agency			

3 Talk about your answers in a small group, and discuss these questions.

    a What other facilities would you like your company to have?
    b Do you think your answers would be different 10 or 15 years from now?

In business | Giving a company tour

Scenario: You have been asked to arrange a tour of your company for some new employees who are starting work soon. First write an email inviting them on the tour, then arrange the tour.

1. Read the invitation email. Complete the gaps so that the invitation comes from you.

Dear _____

I would like to invite you to a tour of the company on _____,
at _____.

We will be meeting in _____ which is down the hall from the cafeteria, the third door on the left.

Please let me know if you can attend this tour as soon as possible.

I look forward to hearing from you soon.

All the best,

_____

---

2. Work with a partner. Choose one of the following types of company (or use your own idea).

Bank	Clothing Company (Head Office)
Bicycle manufacturer	Research Laboratory (Pharmaceuticals)
Sports Club	Your own idea:

3. With your partner, write a list of the most important facilities your company has that new employees will need to know about.

4. Draw a map or floor plan of your company. Include the facilities you would want to show the new employees.

5. Work in a small group. Take it in turns to show the others your map and guide them around your company.

Where's the Marketing Department? **UNIT 8**

Review: Units 5–8

1 Be polite

Change the conversation to make it more polite. Then practise with a partner.

Receptionist:	BL Chemicals.
Kevin:	I want Jon Philpott.
Receptionist:	What's your name?
Kevin:	Kevin Aston, Ashwell Transportation.
Receptionist:	Can't hear. Say it louder.
Kevin:	Kevin Aston. Ashwell Transportation.
Receptionist:	Spell your family name.
Kevin:	A-S-T-O-N.
Receptionist:	Wait.

2 Controlling language

What can you say if …

someone speaks too quietly?

someone speaks too quickly?

you want someone to repeat something?

you want someone to spell something?

3 Conversation map

Use this map to have a telephone conversation with a partner.

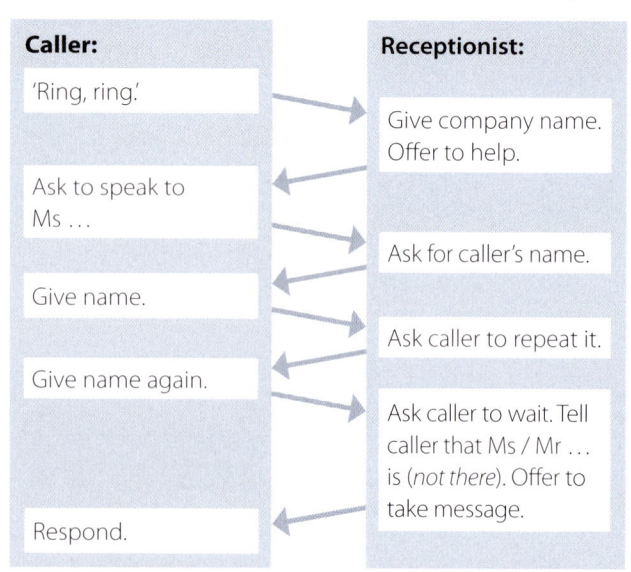

Caller:
- 'Ring, ring.'
- Ask to speak to Ms …
- Give name.
- Give name again.
- Respond.

Receptionist:
- Give company name. Offer to help.
- Ask for caller's name.
- Ask caller to repeat it.
- Ask caller to wait. Tell caller that Ms / Mr … is (not there). Offer to take message.

4 Word square

Hidden in the square are 12 adjectives to describe products. How many words can you find in five minutes? (Look in these directions: ↓ →)

g	e	o	i	s	t	e	n	d	f	r	a
a	w	r	e	l	i	a	b	l	e	q	c
i	d	a	s	e	p	s	l	i	t	u	o
b	s	t	m	e	r	y	x	g	t	f	m
t	t	x	a	y	r	r	n	h	i	s	p
e	r	n	l	i	w	s	j	t	u	t	a
a	o	d	l	e	t	t	i	k	v	i	c
a	n	u	e	f	f	i	c	i	e	n	t
r	g	o	w	f	t	s	e	v	l	o	d
t	z	k	s	s	b	u	f	l	a	s	p
e	h	e	a	v	y	r	a	v	i	c	e
n	o	f	f	l	i	k	s	c	o	h	e
m	a	t	t	r	a	c	t	i	v	e	g
u	r	d	l	u	s	h	a	n	e	a	t
d	e	l	i	c	i	o	u	s	i	p	s

5 What's the difference?

Use the adjectives in exercise 4 to compare the products. Which do you like better? Why?

6 to or about?

Complete the expressions with *to* or *about*. Then read them out loud with a partner.

I'm calling…

a _____ confirm my reservation.
b _____ my visit tomorrow.
c _____ change our meeting time.
d _____ your order #43256.
e _____ our appointment this afternoon.
f _____ ask if we can meet.
g _____ request some information.
h _____ lunch today.

7 Are you free on Monday?

Practise with a partner. Use this conversation map and use your own names.

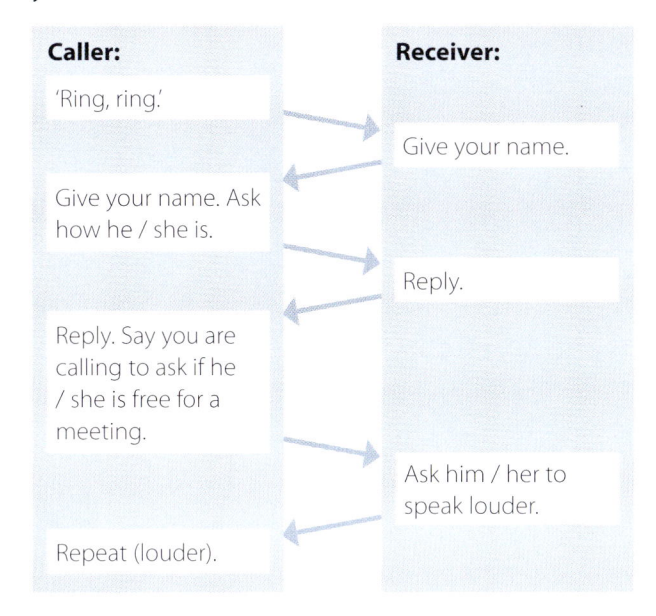

Caller:	Receiver:
'Ring, ring.'	
	Give your name.
Give your name. Ask how he / she is.	
	Reply.
Reply. Say you are calling to ask if he / she is free for a meeting.	
	Ask him / her to speak louder.
Repeat (louder).	

8 Where's the bank?

Add these places to the map:

bank   cinema   chemist   post office

Then take turns giving a tour to other people.

Review **UNITS 5–8** 57

UNIT 9 How long does the process take?

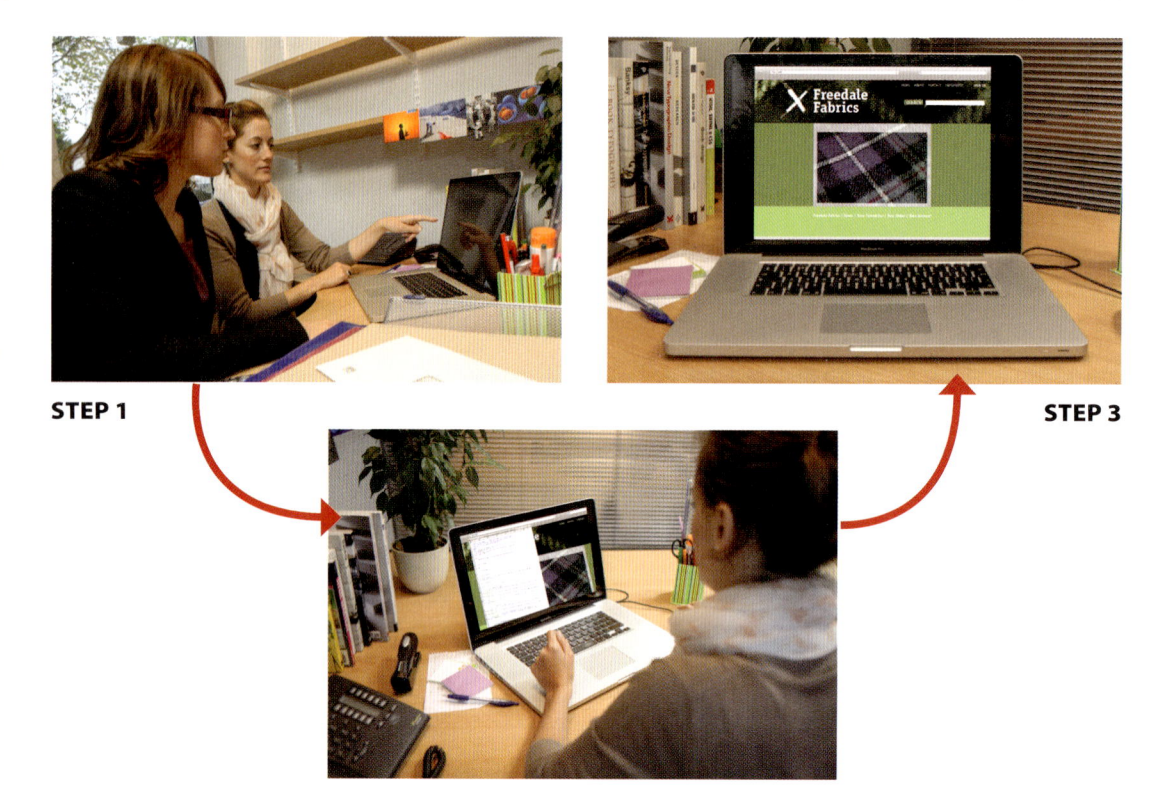

Aims

- Describing a process: sequencing
- Ordering a product
- Checking and confirming
- Recruiting
- Viewpoints: Looking for a job
- In business: Design a process

STEP 1

STEP 2

STEP 3

Listen and practise Sequencing

1 Describe the photos. What is happening? What are they doing?

2 1.50 Helen is describing a web design process to Sven and Jin Soo. Listen and write T for true or F for false next to each sentence.

a   The first step is planning the design. _____
b   The final step is to launch the web page. _____

3 1.50 Listen again and complete the conversation. Then practise with two partners. Take turns being Sven, Jin Soo, and Helen.

Helen: _____ _____ talk to the customers or users of the web page. This is the most important step, to find out what the customer needs. _____ _____, we plan the basic design of the web page. _____ _____ layout of text, graphics, and languages.

Sven: I see. And what do you do next?

Helen: The _____ _____ is we pilot the web page and get feedback from customers.

Jin Soo: Yes, customer feedback is very important.

Helen: _____ we get feedback we revise the design and make any changes or improvements. _____ _____ launch the new web page. Are there any questions?

58 UNIT 9 Get Ready for International Business

4 🔊 1.51 What questions do you think Sven and Jin Soo will ask? Tick (✓) your guesses. Then listen to see if you are correct.

a ☐ How long does the process take?
b ☐ What colour is the web page?
c ☐ Who are the customers?
d ☐ How much does it cost?

Describing a process Sequencing

1 Look at the table. It shows ways you can describe the steps in a process.

First	After (that)…
Second	Before…
Third	Next…
Fourth	Then…
………	At the same time…
	Finally…

The (first) step is…

2 Look at these flow charts. Practise with a partner. Take turns describing the processes.

Begin like this: *There are ___ steps in this process. First you…*

a) A cup of tea

Heat the water. → Put a tea bag in the cup. → Pour boiling water into the cup. → Wait for 3–4 minutes. → Take out the tea bag. → Add milk and sugar if needed.

b) A mango smoothie

Peel and chop the fruit. → Add the fruit to the blender. → Add ice cubes and some yogurt. → Blend for about 1 minute. → Pour the smoothie into glasses.

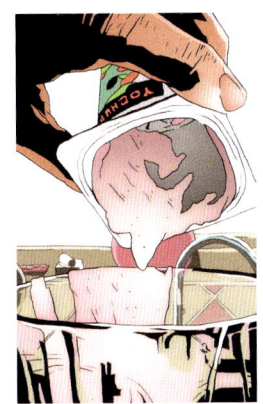

Describing a process Ordering a product

1 Write these sentences under the illustrations.

We send an invoice.   We enter the data.   We order the product from the factory.
We check the inventory.   We arrange delivery.   We receive the order.

2 🔊 1.52 Then listen to Ella and check your answers.

1. We receive the order.
2. We enter the data.
3. We check the inventory.
4. We order the product from the factory.
5. We arrange delivery.
6. We send an invoice.

3 With a partner, use the sentences in exercise 1 to order the steps in the flow chart.

Customer order process

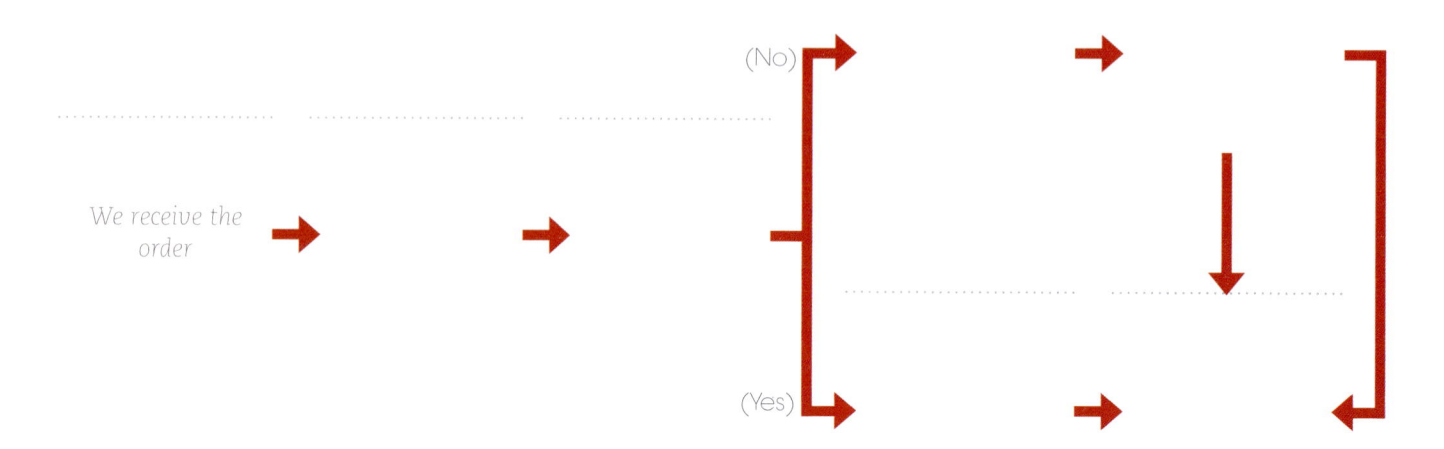

We receive the order

4 🔊 1.52 Listen again. Next to each step write down the sequencing language Ella uses.

5 Now describe the process to a partner. You can use the same language as Ella or you can change some of the language.

Conversation strategy review Checking and confirming

1 Look at the tables. They show ways you can check and confirm understanding.

Is that clear (so far)?	Yes, that's clear.
Are you with me (so far)?	I understand / I'm with you.
OK?	OK.
	Let me confirm that, …
	Let me repeat that, …

2 Choose one of the following and describe it to a partner. Remember to check and confirm the information.

How to use a mobile phone camera

How to make a photocopy

How to boil an egg

How to shampoo and condition your hair

How to brush your teeth

(your idea)

Describing a process Recruiting

Work in a group. Using these steps, describe a recruiting process. Choose one option from Steps 1, 2, and 3.

Begin like this: *There are four steps in our recruiting process. First we …*

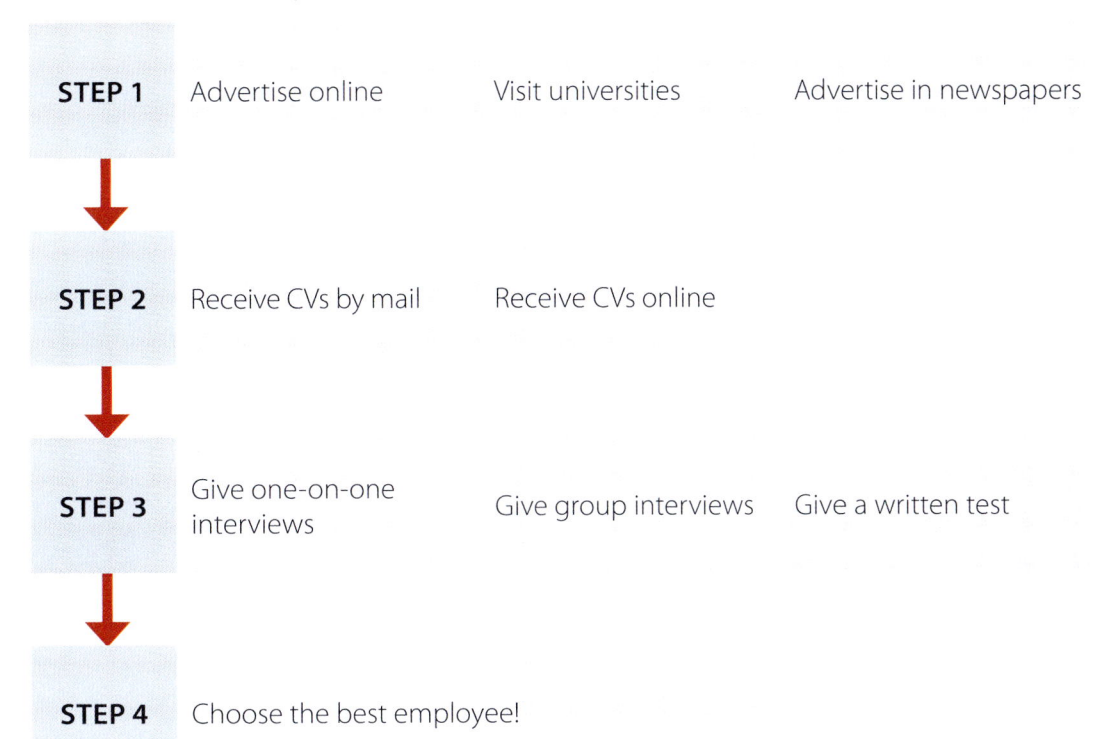

STEP 1   Advertise online   Visit universities   Advertise in newspapers

STEP 2   Receive CVs by mail   Receive CVs online

STEP 3   Give one-on-one interviews   Give group interviews   Give a written test

STEP 4   Choose the best employee!

Talk business

Student A, turn to page 92.

Student B, turn to page 104.

How long does the process take? **UNIT 9** **61**

Viewpoints Looking for a job

1 🔊 1.53 Listen to people from three countries talking about how they looked for a job. Match the person with what they say.

- [ ] It takes about a year!
- [ ] I talked to my professor and he recommended an internship.
- [ ] I went to 15 or 20 interviews.

a Junko Saito, Designer, Japan

b Jean Durand, Engineer, France

c Susan Russell, Manager Trainee, US

- [ ] I looked on the internet.
- [ ] After I graduated the company offered me a job.
- [ ] You can't get experience without a job!

2 🔊 1.53 Now listen again and tick (✓) what method each person used to look for a job.

	Junko	Jean	Susan
Attended job fair			
Visited university job centre			
Friend's advice / recommendation			
Newspaper advertisement			
Professor's advice / recommendation			
Internet / website			

3 How do people in your country look for jobs after college or university? Talk about your answers in a small group.

UNIT 9 Get Ready for International Business

In business | Design a process

Scenario: Your company would like to improve efficiency by making a clear process that everyone will follow. Map it out with your team and present it to the group.

1. Choose from these following ideas the process you are going to design.
   - How products are ordered
   - How new product is developed
   - How new employees are recruited
   - Your own idea _____

2. Map out the process below in groups or pairs.

   Process: _____

3. Work with a new partner or group. Describe your process and check/confirm understanding. After you have finished, repeat the exercise with another partner or group.

UNIT 10 Exports increased sharply

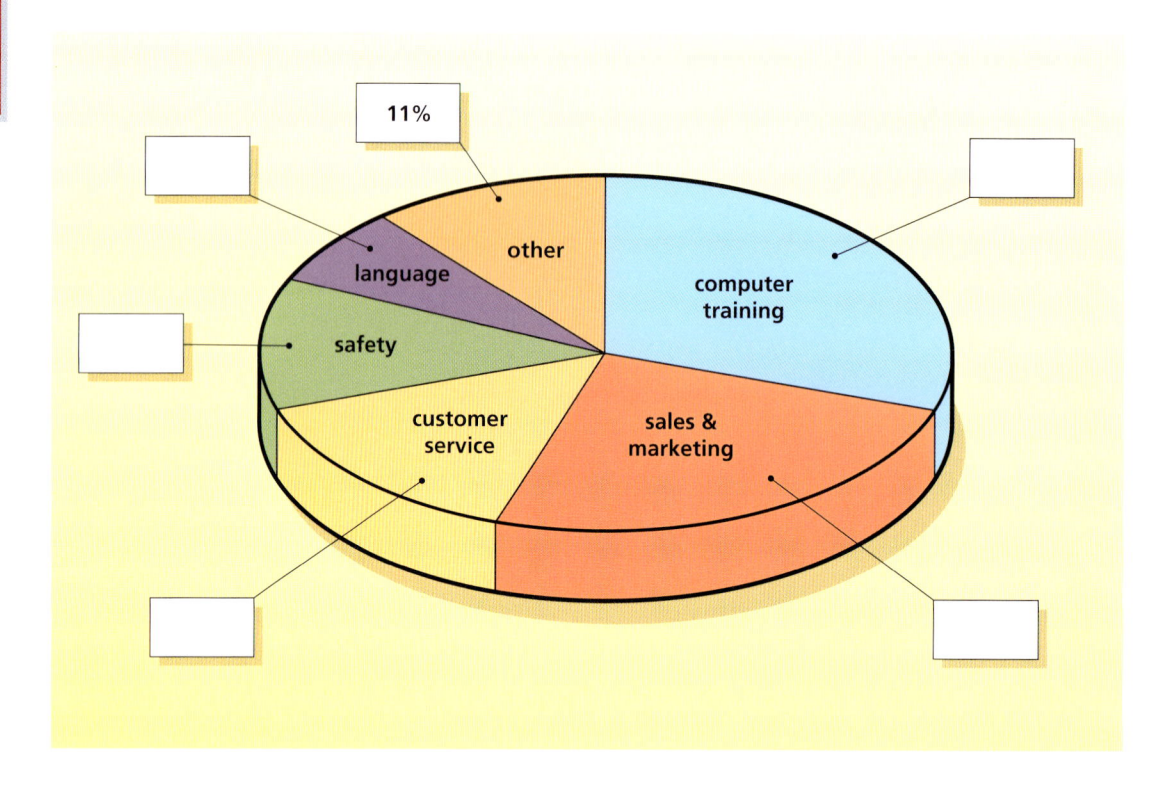

Aims
- Talking about data
- Talking about graphs
- Giving a presentation
- Answering questions
- Viewpoints: Presentations
- In business: Give a presentation

Listen and practise Talking about data

1 Look at the pie chart. What does it show?

2 2.01 Listen to Eduardo's presentation to the Marketing Department. What is the presentation about? Circle the correct answer.

a How to use the new computer system.
b How to spend money for training.
c Why language training is too expensive.

3 2.01 Listen again and complete the pie chart with the correct numbers.

4 Practise with a partner. Change the information in blue using the ideas in the pie chart. Take turns explaining the pie chart.

They spent 35 percent of the training budget on computers.

5 2.02 What do you think Eduardo will do next? Tick (✓) your guesses. Then listen to see if you are correct.

a ☐ He will suggest that everyone take a break.
b ☐ He will talk about next year's training needs.
c ☐ He will talk about how much money the company has now.
d ☐ He will check to see if anyone has any questions.

Talking about graphs

1 Look at the bar graph. What does it show? Why do you think the information is presented in a graph?

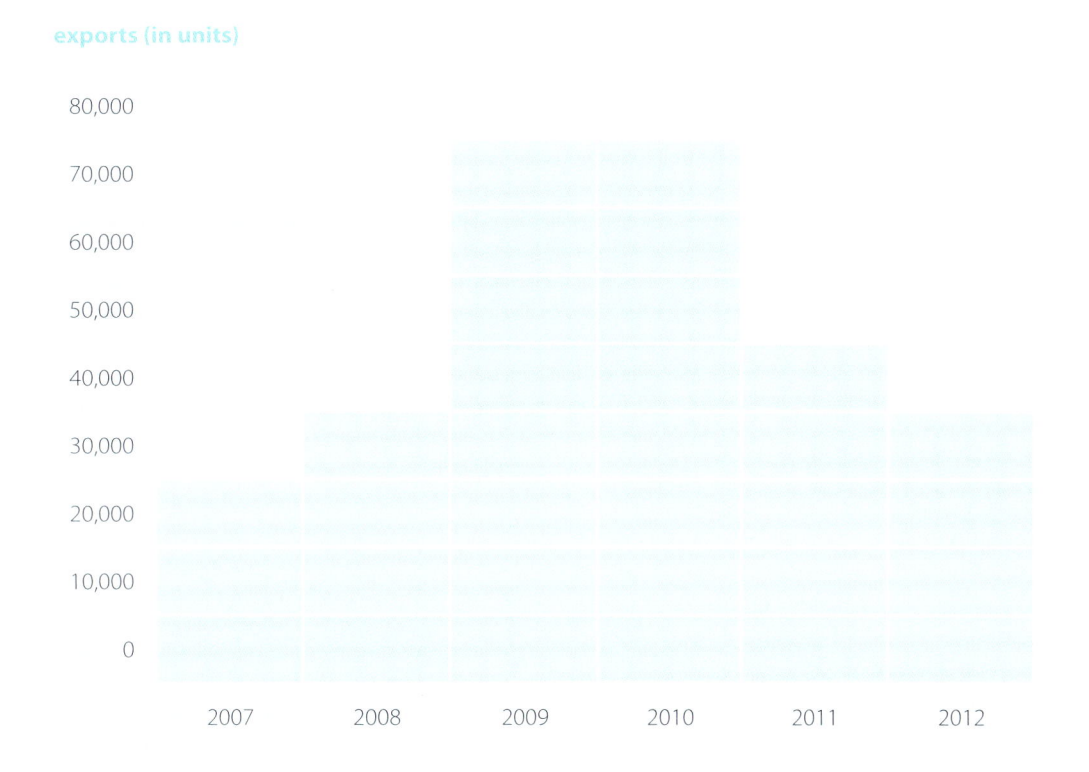

exports (in units)

2 Look at the table. It shows ways you can talk about information in a graph. Look at the bar graph in exercise 1 again, and write the correct year in the table. Then take turns reading the sentences with a partner.

Exports	increased	sharply / slightly	in _2009_
	decreased	sharply / slightly	from _____ to _____ in _____
	stayed about the same from _____ to _____		

3 🔊 Listen to Andrea giving a presentation about the number of customer complaints her department received last year. Draw in the correct bars on the graph.

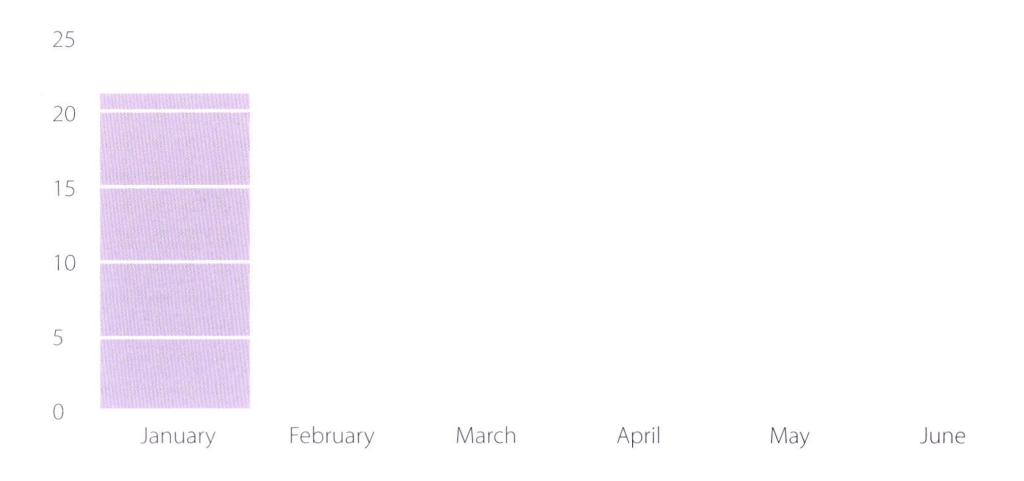

Exports increased sharply **UNIT 10** **65**

Giving a presentation

1 Look at these sentences that people use when they give presentations. When do you think people say them? Copy the sentences into the correct place in the table.

- *OK, can everybody see?*
- *Is everybody here?*
- *Is everybody with me so far?*
- *We're finished for today.*
- *Let's get started.*
- *Let's take a five-minute break.*
- *As you can see here, …*
- *That's all for now.*
- *Thanks for listening. Are there any questions?*

At the beginning	In the middle	At the end

2 2.04 Listen to the presentations. Tick (✓) the sentences you hear.

a ☐ Let's get started.
☐ We'll begin at 10:00.

b ☐ As you can see here, …
☐ Can everybody see?

c ☐ Are there any questions so far?
☐ Is everybody with me so far?

d ☐ That's all for today.
☐ I think we're finished.

Talk business
Student A, turn to page 93.
Student B, turn to page 105.

Answering questions

1 🔊 2.05 After a presentation, we often ask our audience if there are any questions. But what happens if you don't know the answer? Listen to these ways you can respond. Then practise with a partner.

A: Excuse me, how much will the new computers cost?
B: **I'm sorry, I'm not really sure. I'll check on that and get back to you.**
A: Thanks, I'd appreciate that.

A: When is the next training session?
B: **I'm sorry, I don't know. I'll check with** Pam **and let you know.**
A: OK, thanks.

A: Is this information available in a document?
B: **Actually, I'm not sure. Let me check on that for you.**
A: Oh, that's OK, it's not important.

2 Work with a partner. Take turns asking the questions and responding. Use the conversations in exercise 1 as models.

a What's the population of Russia?
b Who is the Prime Minister of Australia?
c How much does an average apartment in Paris cost?
d When was the internet invented?
e How many people speak Mandarin?
f What are the official languages of Sri Lanka?
g What is the CEO's salary?
h How many employees are there in Taiwan?

Viewpoints Presentations

1 Read what these people say about giving and attending presentations. Which kinds of presentations have you given or attended?

Mei-ling Chen, Project Manager, Singapore

We have customers from many different companies, so our presentations are in English. We use a lot of charts and graphs to make sure everyone understands the information. Some of our presentations are pretty long, so we sometimes take a tea break in the middle.

Tasha Green, Administrative Assistant, US

These days, most people use some kind of presentation software like PowerPoint®. Sometimes the presentations look really good, but I don't like it when people just read their slides to you. That's boring.

Viktor Brodsky, CEO, Ukraine

I prefer to just talk during my presentations. I don't want to worry about using equipment and graphs and charts. If you depend on equipment and it doesn't work, then what happens to your presentation?

2 Which kinds of presentations do you like? Put a tick (✓) on the bar closest to your opinion. Then talk about your opinions in a group. (If you haven't attended or given any presentations, answer about a school class.)

no opinion; either is fine
⬇

I like long presentations.	I like short presentations.
It's OK if I don't know the topic in advance.	I want to know the topic in advance.
Eating and drinking is distracting.	I like to drink coffee or tea, or have a snack.
Only the presenter should talk.	Everyone should give their opinions.
The atmosphere should be formal. I don't like a lot of joking around.	I like an informal atmosphere. It's OK if the presenter tells some jokes.
People should ask questions at the end of the presentation.	People should ask questions whenever they think of them.
I like just listening during a presentation – no visual aids.	I prefer some kind of visual aid, like PowerPoint® or a graph or chart.

In business: Give a presentation

Scenario: You have been asked to give a presentation to a visiting group of people from a company in Brazil. Prepare and give your presentation.

1. Choose some information about your company that you would like to present.
   - Sales figures from one year
   - Sales figures from more than one year
   - Types of products that your company has
   - The budget for one department
   - The number of imports or exports over a period of several months or years
   - The number of employees who work in each department in your company
   - The number or type of customer complaints
   - Your own idea

2. Draw a pie chart or a graph to present your information. Use this space or design it on a computer.

3. Work in groups or with the whole class. Take turns giving a presentation. Don't forget to start and end your presentation with the language on page 66, and to check understanding during your presentation. After you have listened to your classmates' presentations, ask them questions.

Exports increased sharply **UNIT 10**

UNIT 11

I'm leaving tomorrow

Aims

- Confirming next steps
- Talking about future plans
- Degrees of certainty
- Viewpoints: Talking about the future
- In business: Describe future plans

Listen and practise   Confirming next steps

1 Describe the photos. What is happening?

2 2.06 Scott and Andrew are meeting. Listen to the conversation. Write T for true or F for false next to each sentence.

   a   Scott will send the contract by the 5th.
   b   Andrew is leaving this weekend.

3 2.06 Listen again and complete the conversation. Then practise with a partner. Take turns being Scott and Andrew.

   Scott: OK, let me confirm our next steps. _____ send us a
             cost estimate by the end of this week. Is that right?
   Andrew: That's right, and _____ prepare the contract?
   Scott: Yes, we'll send it to you by the 15th. Is that OK?
   Andrew: That's great. _____ working on this right away.
   Scott: Great! _____ back this weekend?
   Andrew: Yes, I'm leaving tomorrow morning.
   Scott: What _____ this evening?
   Andrew: Nothing special. I'm going to pack my suitcases.

4 Practise the conversation again. Change the information in blue using the ideas below.

   a   deliver the parts this afternoon / prepare the invoice / by Friday
   b   arrange a meeting by the 12th / make the agenda / by tomorrow
   c   meet the customer tomorrow / check the address / today
   d   finish the report by five o'clock / send the data / by lunchtime

5 ◼ 2.07 What do you think Scott will say next? Tick (✓) your guesses. Then listen to see if you are correct.

a ☐ Where is your hotel? c ☐ How many suitcases do you have?
b ☐ Have a good flight! d ☐ Would you like to have dinner?

Talking about future plans

1 Look at the table. It shows ways you can talk about future plans.

Form	Example	Meaning
will	I will finish the report tomorrow.	intention, promise
	Don't worry, I'll help you.	just decided
be going to	We're going to meet him today.	already planned
verb + -ing	I'm leaving tomorrow.	already planned (usually near future)

2 ◼ 2.08 Listen to these five conversations. Match the conversation with the picture. Number the pictures in order 1–5.

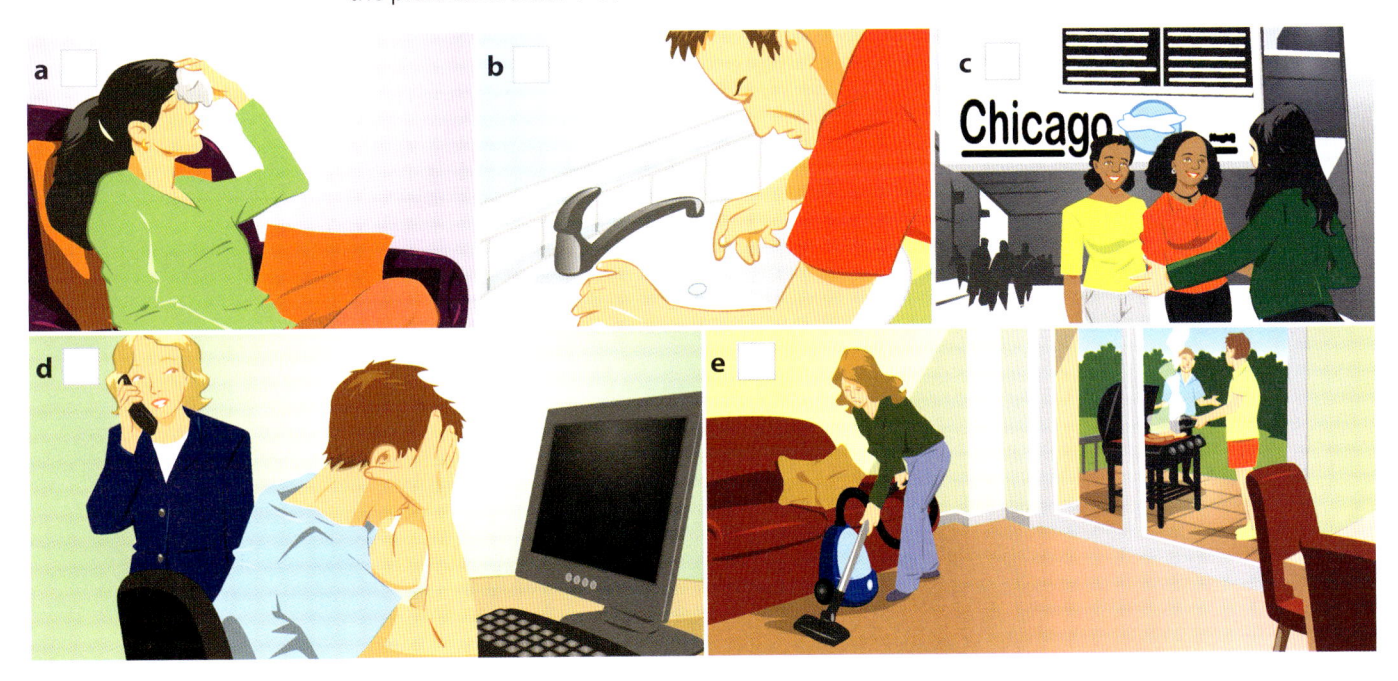

3 ◼ 2.08 Listen again and complete these sentences from the conversations. Check your answers with a partner.

a Don't worry, _I'll help_ you find it. (help)
b 6:30. _____ a taxi to the airport. (take)
c My friends _____ at the airport. (meet)
d I'm too tired. _____ tomorrow. (go shopping)
e Tomorrow _____ a barbecue. (have)
f On Sunday _____ my flat. (clean up)
g I'm not sure. Perhaps _____ a film. (watch)
h Just a minute, _____ the help desk. (call)

I'm leaving tomorrow **UNIT 11** **71**

4 Look at the table. It shows ways you can ask about future plans. With a partner, ask about future plans. Then change partners and repeat the exercise.

	tomorrow?
What are you going to do	next week?
What are you doing	tonight?
	next Sunday?

5 Here are some other verbs you can use to talk about future plans. With a different partner, talk about your plans for three, five, and ten years from now.

For example:

Five years from now I hope to work in France.

		plan to	
Three years from now,	I	am planning to	visit London.
			buy a house.
		hope to	be the Sales Manager.
		am hoping to	

6 2.09 Listen and draw lines to connect the company with their plans. Describe the plans. Then check your answers with a partner.

Talk business

Student A, turn to page 94.

Student B, turn to page 106.

a   Marco Supermarkets   increase sales in Asia   next year
b   Ruhr Pipe Manufacturing   open four more stores   this year
c   Timson Watches   hire more staff   in the next two years
d   Aztec Coffee   build a new plant   three years from now

Degrees of certainty

1 Look at the table. It shows adverbs you can use to show how certain we are about something.

definitely	definitely not	stronger
probably	probably not	↓
perhaps / maybe	perhaps not / maybe not	weaker

2 In groups of three, ask and answer these questions.

For example: A: *Do you think it'll rain tomorrow?*
B: *Maybe. How about you?*
A: *Probably not. What do you think?*
C: *Definitely not.*

1 Do you think it'll rain next weekend?
2 Do you think you'll travel overseas next year?
3 Do you think you'll work for a big company?

3 Look at these sentences; they show the position of the adverb. Practise saying them with a partner.

I'll **definitely** send the invoice today.

We're **probably** going to visit Malaysia next week.

Perhaps I'll take a day off tomorrow.
Maybe I'll visit New York next year.
Do you think you'll visit the factory next week? I **probably** will.

I **definitely** won't finish the report today.

We're **probably** not going to the meeting next week.

4 How sure are you about these statements? Talk about your answers in a group.

a   I'll live overseas.
b   I'll run a marathon next year. 
c   In five years I'll be on TV. 
d   I'll use English in my job. 

I'm leaving tomorrow UNIT 11

Viewpoints: Talking about the future

1 🔊 2.10 Listen to people from three different countries talking about their futures. Write down the degree of certainty next to their plans.

Ji-young Kim,
Office Worker, Korea

Amnuay Chaichan,
Assistant Sales Manager, Thailand

Julie Howe,
Construction Worker, Canada

I'll _definitely_ stay with this company.
I'll _____ be sent to the US to study.
_____ I will be a manager.
I'll _____ get married sometime.
I _____ want to continue working after I'm married.

I'll _____ travel around Europe.
I _____ want to take my family with me.

_____ I'll work in the US for a few years.
I _____ want to come back to Canada.

2 In groups of three, pretend you are one of the people in exercise 1. Tell the others about your future plans.

3 Do you know what you want to do in the future? What are some of your future hopes, plans, and dreams? Make some notes in the table below. Talk about your future plans in a small group.

Time frame	Event / Action

UNIT 11 Get Ready for International Business

In business Describe future plans

Scenario: You have been asked to give a presentation to investors in your company about your plans for the future.

1. Work with a partner or in groups of three. Choose one of the following industries (or use your own idea).

Car Manufacturing	Cosmetics	Cellphone Manufacturing
Fast-food Restaurants	E-learning: English online	Your own idea:

2. With your partner or group, decide what kind of company it is (for example, how many employees you have, what type of products you sell or make, where your head office is, how many offices you have).

3. Think about how your company will change over the next three, five and ten years. Discuss these questions and make notes.
   - Are you going to expand your business?
   - Are you going to open overseas offices?
   - Are you going to hire more people?
   - Are you planning to make different products?

4. Complete the table below with your ideas. You may also like to make some graphs and charts to show your ideas.

Time frame	Event / Action

5. Present your plans to your group or class. Begin like this:

   Thanks for coming today. I'm going to talk about our future plans. First …

I'm leaving tomorrow **UNIT 11**

UNIT 12 Would you like to try some dim sum?

Aims
- Entertaining guests
- Offering and accepting or refusing food
- Giving and receiving compliments
- Thanking and responding to thanks
- Viewpoints: Food and business entertaining
- In business: Planning a social event

Listen and practise — Entertaining guests

1 Describe the photo.

2 Listen to some business people entertaining their guests. Tick (✓) the foods and drinks they mention.

☐ chicken   ☐ coffee   ☐ salad
☐ vegetables   ☐ shrimp   ☐ tea

3 Listen again and complete the conversation. Then practise with a partner. Take turns being Lily and Grace.

Lily: _____ you _____ to try some dim sum?
Grace: Yes, thank you, they _____ delicious. Um, what's _____ them?
Lily: These ones have _____ , and these ones have _____ .
Grace: And, uh, _____ do I eat them?
Lily: Oh, it's _____ . You _____ one _____ with your chopsticks… like this… and dip it into the sauce.

4 Practise the conversation again. Change the information in blue using the ideas below.

a   tacos / beef, beans and cheese / hand / just eat it
b   samosas / potatoes, meat / fork / put it on your plate
c   sushi / cucumber, fish / chopsticks / dip it in soy sauce

---

76   UNIT 12   Get Ready for International Business

5 What do you think Lily will do next? Tick (✓) your guesses. Then listen to see if you are correct.

a ☐ She will offer Grace something to drink.
b ☐ She will ask Grace if she likes the dim sum.
c ☐ She will tell Grace how to make dim sum.
d ☐ She will ask Grace to pass her some food.

Offering and accepting or refusing food

1 Look at the tables. They show ways you can offer food, and accept or refuse food. Practise with a partner. Take turns reading the questions and answers.

Questions:

Would you like to try*	a taco?
Would you like	a cup of coffee? some crisps? some (more) cake?

*(**Note:** Use **to try** if your guest has not had the food before.)

Answers:

Yes, please.	It looks They smell That sounds	delicious. wonderful. good.
No, thank you.	I just had one / some. I can't eat any more!	
	I'm	a vegetarian. allergic. on a diet.

2 Listen to these conversations. Tick (✓) the question that you hear. Then write the response.

a ☐ Would you like some …?
  ☐ Would you like to try some …?

b ☐ Would you like some more …?
  ☐ Would you like to try some …?

c ☐ Would you like a …?
  ☐ Would you like some …?

d ☐ Would you like some …?
  ☐ Would you like some more …?

3 Practise with a partner. Take turns offering these foods and drinks and accepting or refusing them. Use the information below and your own ideas.

a   some pizza

c   some chicken curry

b   a brownie

d   an apple

Giving and receiving compliments

1 2.14 Listen to the conversations.

Conversation 1

Guest: This fish is delicious!
Host: No, it isn't. It's too salty and dry.
Guest: Oh. Well, it tastes good to me …

Conversation 2

Guest: This curry is delicious!
Host: Oh, thank you. My daughter made it with me. I hope it's not too spicy.
Guest: No, not at all. What's in it?
Host: Well, chicken, fresh vegetables, and my own spices. Would you like the recipe?
Guest: Yes, thank you. That's very kind of you.

2 Discuss these questions with a partner.

a   In which conversation does the guest feel uncomfortable? Why? Practise the successful conversation.

b   In English, it is common to give compliments. If you receive a compliment, it is polite to accept it (*Thank you*) and then say one or two more sentences about the item that is being complimented (*My daughter made it with me. I hope it's not too spicy.*). What is the custom in your culture?

(**Note:** Do not give compliments on a person's personal appearance. You might hurt someone's feelings, or give the wrong impression. Women can compliment other women on their clothing or accessories, but men should not give these kinds of compliments to women.)

Talk business

Student A, turn to page 95.

Student B, turn to page 107.

3 Practise with a partner. Take turns giving and accepting compliments. Use the information below and then your own ideas. Use a polite tone of voice!

a   garden is lovely / wife planted the roses

c   coffee is delicious / from Guatemala

b   town is beautiful / many old buildings

d   son is very smart / only two years old

Thanking and responding to thanks

1 Look at the table. Then practise with a partner. Take turns thanking and responding.

Thank you for	lunch	You're welcome.
	the flowers.	I'm glad you liked it / them.
	inviting me.	Oh, don't mention it.
	sending me the report.	Oh, not at all.

2 Work in a group. Take turns thanking every group member for something. Respond to your classmates' thanks in a different way each time.

Thank you for being my partner.   You're welcome.

Thank you for making me laugh.   Oh, don't mention it.

Would you like to try some dim sum?   **UNIT 12**   **79**

Viewpoints Food and business entertaining

1 Read what these people from around the world say about food. Which culture is most similar to yours?

Rajiv Das, Business man, India

Business lunches are more common than business dinners. If you are served traditional Indian food, remember to eat only with the right hand – even if you are left-handed! In addition, do not use your hands to take food from a communal dish. Muslims do not eat pork, and Hindus do not eat beef, so vegetarian dishes are common.

Dmitri Petrov, Product Planner, Russia

Russians appreciate a good supply of different snacks and drinks at business meetings. Both the food and the serving dishes (plates, cups, and so on) should be of good quality. If you are invited to a Russian's home, you will be offered a lot of food! It is polite to bring a gift if you are the guest.

Lucia Dominguez, CEO, Argentina

Business entertaining is very common. We usually invite guests to dinner at a restaurant, not a private home. We don't talk about business over dinner, though – it's a time to get to know one another on a social level. Meat, especially local beef, is a popular dish. Dinners start at around 10:00pm.

2 What kind of foods do you like to eat on these occasions? Make a quick list.

for breakfast	while watching TV	for dessert	when I'm unhappy	at a birthday party	at a sporting event

3 Compare your answers in a group. How would you explain any foods that an international visitor would not know? Tell the group. Do you all enjoy the same kinds of food?

In business: Planning a social event

Scenario: You have been asked by your boss to plan a social event for your company.

1 Discuss the following questions in a group.
- What is the reason for the party?
- Who will you invite?
- What kind of entertainment will you have?
- What kind of food will you serve?

snacks	food	drinks

Report back your ideas to the group or class.

2 Role-play your party in a group or with the whole class. Use this conversation map.

Host:
- Offer some food or drink.
- If the guest refuses, offer something else until the guest accepts.
- Accept the compliment and give more information.
- Accept the thanks.
- Say goodbye.

Guest:
- Accept or Refuse (say why).
- Compliment the food or drink.
- Thank the host.
- Say goodbye.

Would you like to try some dim sum? **UNIT 12** 81

Review: Units 9–12

1 Where's it from?

Match the food to the country. Then use the conversation map to offer and accept.

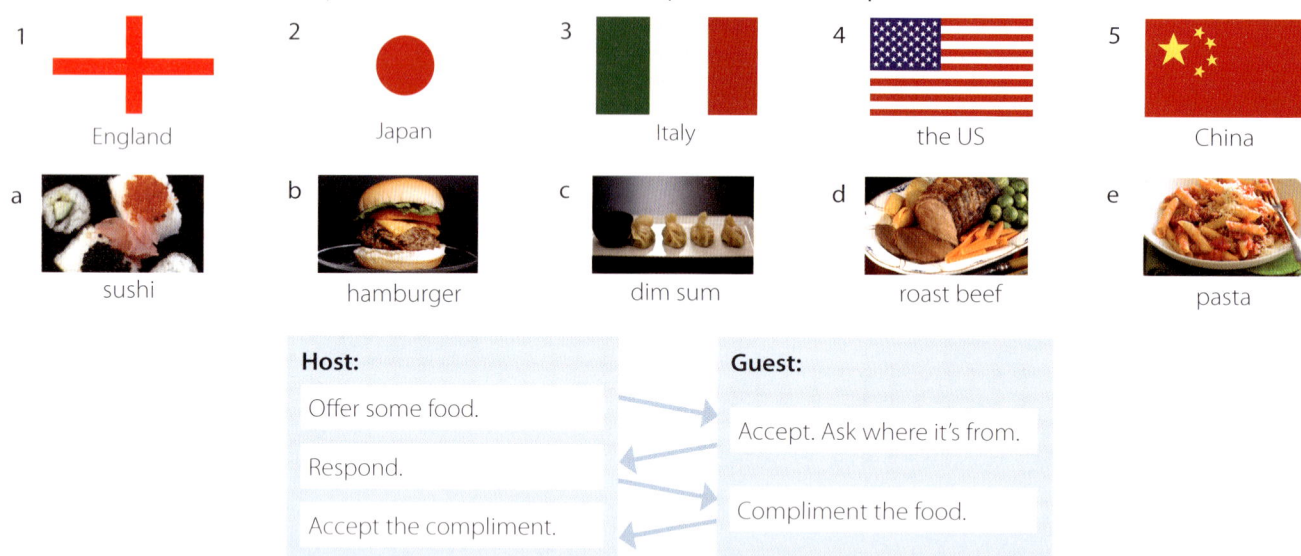

1 England 2 Japan 3 Italy 4 the US 5 China

a sushi b hamburger c dim sum d roast beef e pasta

Host:
- Offer some food.
- Respond.
- Accept the compliment.

Guest:
- Accept. Ask where it's from.
- Compliment the food.

2 Finish the graph!

Complete the graph and add a title. Describe the graph to a partner.

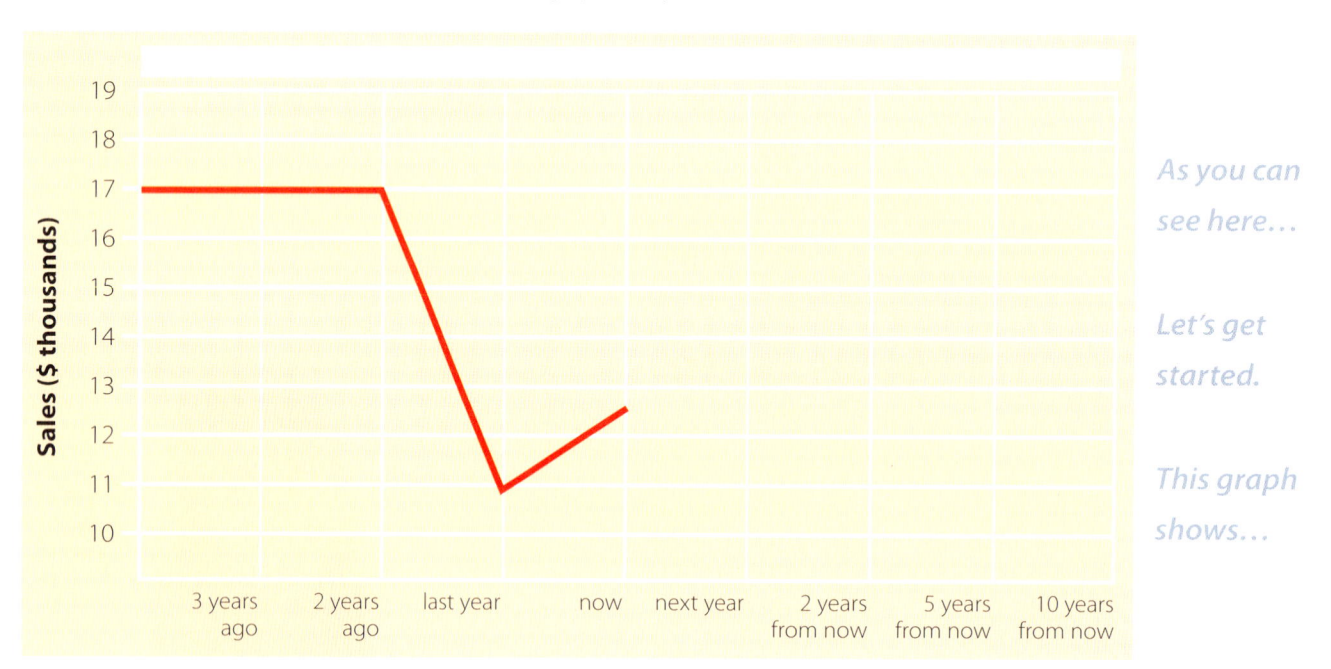

Sales ($ thousands)

3 years ago | 2 years ago | last year | now | next year | 2 years from now | 5 years from now | 10 years from now

As you can see here…

Let's get started.

This graph shows…

3 What's the next step?

2.15 Listen and complete the steps in the process. Then describe the process to a partner.

a c _____ o _____
b m _____ t _____ g
c t _____ n _____
d s _____ g

82 UNITS 9–12 Get Ready for International Business

4 Great job!

Match the compliment with the response. Then practise with a partner.

a I enjoyed your presentation!   Thank you. We moved here last month.
b I like your bag!   Thank you! They're chocolate chip. My daughter made them.
c These are nice offices!   Thank you. It was a present from my mother.
d These are delicious!   Thank you! It took me a long time to make the slides.

5 Q&A

With a partner ask and answer questions about the graph.
Then student A gives an answer, and student B makes the question.

For example:
Q *How many people joined FM Fashion last year?*
A *102.*

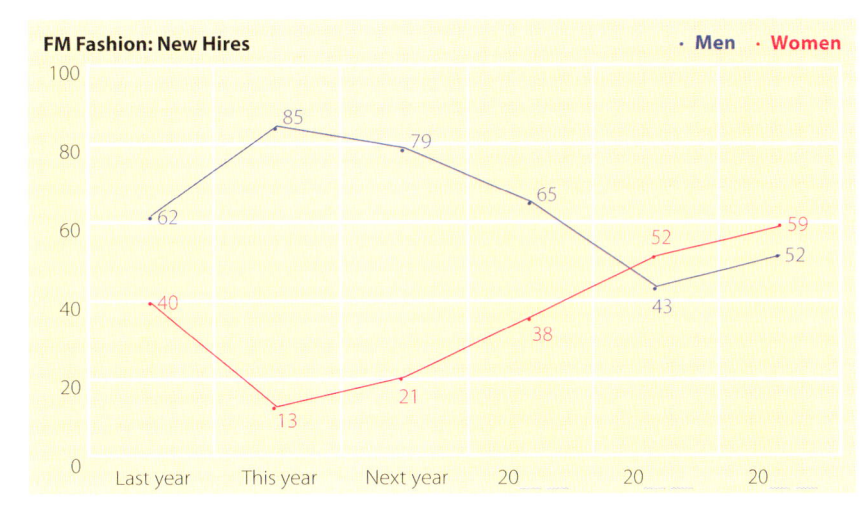

For example:
A *38.*
Q *How many women will probably join FM Fashion in 20____?*

6 Don't mention it.

2.16 Jill wants to thank you. Listen and respond when you hear the beep.

7 I'll definitely climb Mt. Everest!

What are your plans for next year? Complete the sentences. Compare your answers with a partner.

Next year	I'll definitely	
	I'll probably	
	perhaps I'll	
	maybe I'll	

Review **UNITS 9–12**

Talk business

Student A: use this page Student B: use page 96

Useful language

What	do	you	do?
Who	are do	you	with work for?
What	is	your	address? postcode? phone number? email address?

1 Ask questions to complete student B's business card below. Write B's responses.

Chris Chandler
production _____

Media Services
We produce top-quality videos

66 _____ Street
Dublin 7
(01) 484 _____
_____ @ _____

2 Answer student B's questions about your business card.

PACIFIC FINANCE

Mary Chan
Marketing Manager

Personal Banking Services

105 Thomson Road ... Tel: 6355 5749
33-05 United Square ... Fax: 6355 6763
Singapore 309875
email: chan_c@pacfinance.com

3 Compare your books. Did you get the correct information?

UNIT 1 Get Ready for International Business

Talk business

Student A: use this page Student B: use page 97

Useful language

Do you	write emails? take part in one-on-one meetings? take part in teleconferences?
How often do you	give presentations? make telephone calls? go on overseas business trips?

1 Ask student B questions to complete the survey about B's on-the-job use of English. Write B's responses.

Asia Research Centre – Survey of on-the-job use of English

Activity	Yes / No	How often?
read emails		
write emails		
take part in one-on-one meetings		
take part in group meetings		
use the telephone		
take part in teleconferences		
give presentations		
go on overseas business trips		
other: *welcome foreign visitors*		

2 Answer student B's questions. Use this information.

Asia Research Centre – Survey of on-the-job use of English

Activity	Yes / No	How often?
read emails	Yes	every day
write emails	Yes	every day
take part in one-on-one meetings	Yes	once a month
take part in group meetings	Yes	two or three times a month
use the telephone	Yes	every day
take part in teleconferences	No	–
give presentations	No	–
go on overseas business trips	No	–
other: *give factory tours*	Yes	every month

3 Compare your books. Did you get the correct information?

Talk business

Student A: use this page Student B: use page 98

Useful language

What		does	your company		do?
Where		is	your head office?		
When		was	the company		established?
How many	offices employees	do	you		have?

1 Ask student B questions to get information about Rock On! Records. Complete the table.

Rock On! Records

Head office:	
Established:	
Employees:	
Offices:	
Factories:	
Business:	

2 Answer student B's questions about Fujimoto Heavy Industries.

Fujimoto Heavy Industries

Head office:	Kawasaki, Japan
Established:	1946
Employees:	32,097
Offices:	Kawasaki, Tokyo, Osaka
Factories:	Kawasaki, Sasebo
Business:	builds ships, makes airplanes

3 Compare your books. Did you get the correct information?

Talk business

Student A: use this page Student B: use page 99

Useful language

You should …	
Why don't you … ?	That's a good idea, thanks.
I recommend …	Well, maybe.
How about … ?	

1 Tell student B your problems. Listen to B's suggestions.

If you like the suggestion, say, 'That's a good idea, thanks.'

If you don't like the suggestion, say, 'Well, maybe.'

a   I feel very sleepy now.
b   I don't understand this word.
c   I want to buy a cheap plane ticket.
d   I usually miss my morning bus.
e   I need some more money.

2 Listen to student B's problems. Make suggestions using the information below.

ride your bicycle to work
give it to me
read the manual

go shopping with me
try to relax more
ask one of your classmates

Talk business **UNIT 4** **87**

Talk business

Student A: use this page Student B: use page 100

Useful language

How do you spell (that)?
Can you speak more slowly?
Can you speak more loudly?

Can you repeat that?
Can you say that again?

1 You are the caller.

You are Chris Patterson at J&B Productions.
Your phone number is 077 – 9888 – 6533.

Call student B and ask for Jennifer Cho. If she is not there, leave a message. Ask her to call you back tomorrow morning.

Begin the call by saying: *'Ring, ring'.*

2 You are the receiver.

You will receive a phone call from student B. You are the receptionist for NBI. Ms Thompson is in a meeting.

Take a message using the form below. Remember to thank the caller and end the phone call!

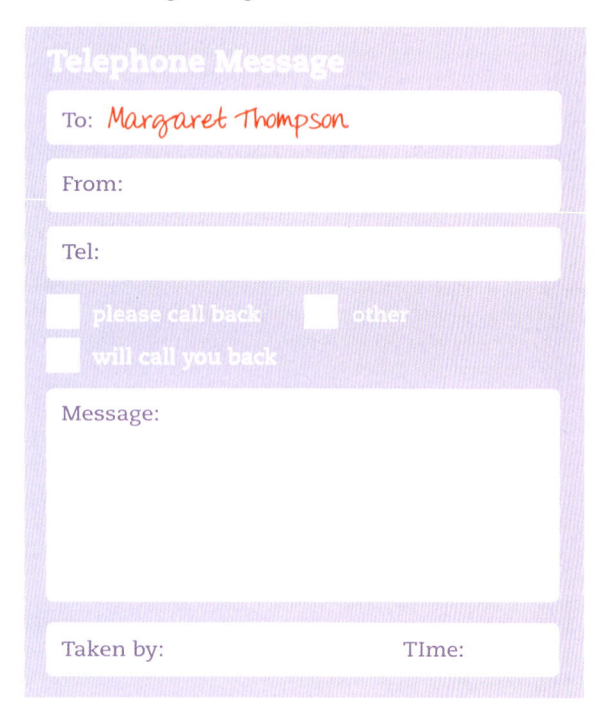

Telephone Message

To: Margaret Thompson

From:

Tel:

☐ please call back   ☐ other
☐ will call you back

Message:

Taken by: **TIme:**

3 Compare your books. Did you get the correct information?

UNIT 5 Get Ready for International Business

Talk business

Student A: use this page   Student B: use page 101

Practise the conversation below. Then have similar conversations using the information in the charts.

A: Do you know which (camera) is (cheaper)?

B: Well, (the XLR) is ($300). How about the (Ricon 900)?

A: That one is ($500).

B: OK, then (the XLR) is (cheaper). You should get that one.

1 Ask shopper B about the smartphone, the English book, and the video game.

Begin like this: *Do you know which smartphone is lighter?*

1 smartphone – light
the Blueberry: ____ grams
the Strawberry: 5 grams

2 English book – short
Great Grammar: ____ pages
Grammar Fun: 128 pages

3 video game – good
Space Battle: ____ stars
Educational Journey: 2 stars

2 Talk with shopper B about the suit, the CD, and the ladder. (B starts.)

4 suit – expensive
the Yugo Moss: $900
the Nolo: $____

5 CD – new
Radio Hits: 20 years old
Hot Hip Hop: ____ years old

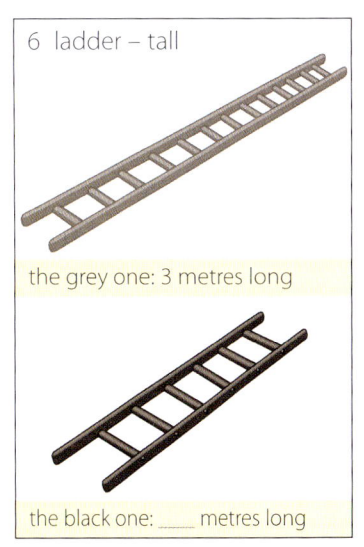

6 ladder – tall
the grey one: 3 metres long
the black one: ____ metres long

3 Compare your books. Did you get the correct information?

Talk business **UNIT 6** **89**

Talk business

Student A: use this page Student B: use page 102

Let me confirm.
Let me repeat that.

That's ... .
You said ... .
The ... is ... .

Is that right?

1 Caller

You are Mary Chan.

You are calling the Pacific Restaurant. You want to make a lunch reservation.

Restaurant: (Student B)
You: Hello, I'd like to make a reservation, please.

This is your reservation information:

12:45 Pacific Restaurant 14th Dec
(5) adults, 3 children
Mobile phone: 075 3333 8570

2 Receiver

You are Anna Martinez at BL Chemicals

You will receive a phone call from Mikel Deuter at Ruhr Pipe. Write down his order in the form. (Remember to check the information!)

You: Hello, BL Chemicals. How can I help you?
Mikel Deuter: (Student B)
You: Certainly. Can you give me the part numbers and quantity, Mr Deuter?
Mikel Deuter: ....
You: Thank you for your order, Mr Deuter. I will send you an email today to confirm this information.

BL Chemicals: Order Form	
Part Number	Quantity

3 Compare your books. Did you get the correct information?

Talk business

Student A: use this page Student B: use page 103

Useful language

Where is the _____?
It's …

across from   behind   between   in front of
in the corner   next to / on the left
next to / on the right   under

1. Look at the map of the shopping centre below. Ask student B where these shops are, and write them onto the map: *ice cream shop, video game arcade, furniture shop, cosmetics shop.*

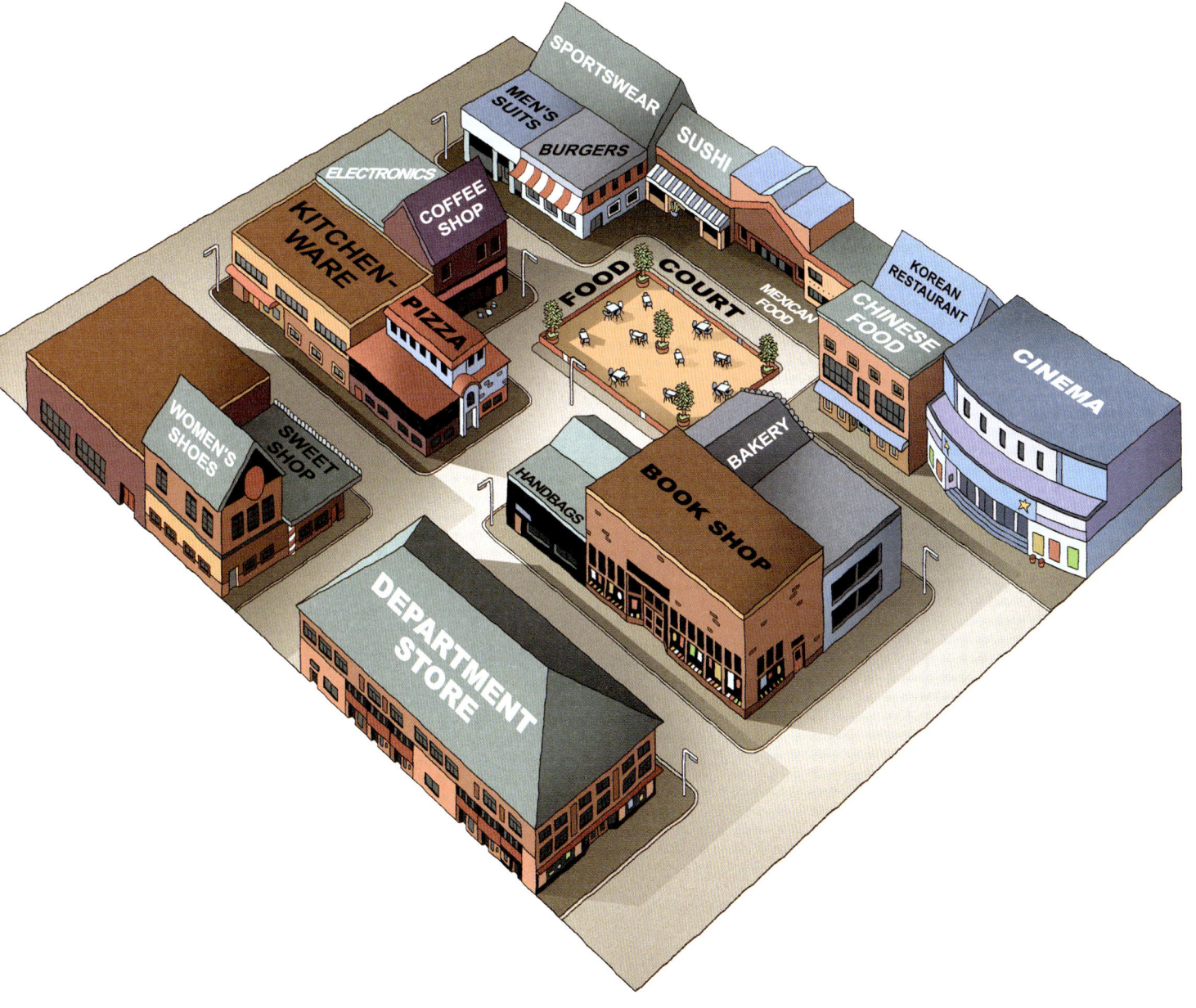

2. Answer student B's questions.

3. Compare your books. Did you get the right information?

Talk business **UNIT 8**   **91**

Talk business

Student A: use this page   Student B: use page 104

1. Describe the first part of the process to student B. Check that he / she understands.

   Begin like this:
   The first step is to research the company.
   For example, what are their products? ...

   Useful language
   Is that clear (so far)?
   Are you with me (so far)?
   OK?

   Preparing for a job interview.

   1 Research the company — What are their products? / Who are their main customers?

   2 Plan your route — Where is the office? / How long does it take to get there?

   3 Practise — Prepare answers: What are your strengths / weaknesses / future dreams?

   4 Dress right — Look professional. / Get a haircut.

2. Listen to student B's description and complete the second part of the process. Check and confirm that you understand.

   Useful language
   Yes, that's clear.
   I understand.
   OK.
   I'm with you.

   Let me repeat that ...
   Let me confirm ...

   5 _____ early — _____ _____ minutes early. / _____ off your mobile phone.

   6 _____ _____ shy! — Talk about your experiences. / _____ _____ who you are!

   7 _____ _____ — Ask about the company and _____ _____. / Ask about _____ plans.

   8 Follow-up — _____ _____ : Send a thank-you note or _____ .

3. Compare your books. Did you get the correct information?

UNIT 9 Get Ready for International Business

Talk business

Student A: use this page Student B: use page 105

Here is information about visitors to the Grand Canyon in Arizona, US.

1 a Complete the pie chart. Ask student B for information like this:

What percentage of visitors to the Grand Canyon were (…)?

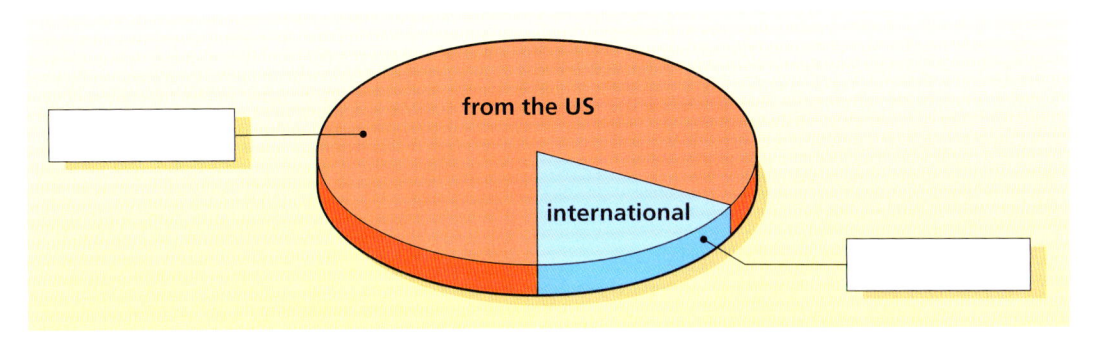

[Pie chart: from the US / international]

b Complete the bar graph by drawing in the correct bars for each country. Ask student B for information like this:

How many people came from (…)?

[Bar graph with y-axis 60–240, countries: United Kingdom, Canada, Japan, Germany, The Netherlands, Australia]

2 Answer student B's questions with this information:

a Most visitors to the Grand Canyon National Park, 58.6 percent, were first-time visitors. 41.4 percent were repeat visitors, or visitors who had been to the park before.

b

State	Number of visitors
California	739
Arizona	535
Texas	288
Florida	204
New York	195
Ohio	190

3 Compare your books. Did you get the correct information?

Talk business

Student A: use this page Student B: use page 106

Useful language

From January to February we
In March we

will …
are going to …
plan to …
hope to …

1 Describe the development schedule to student B. Check that he / she understands.

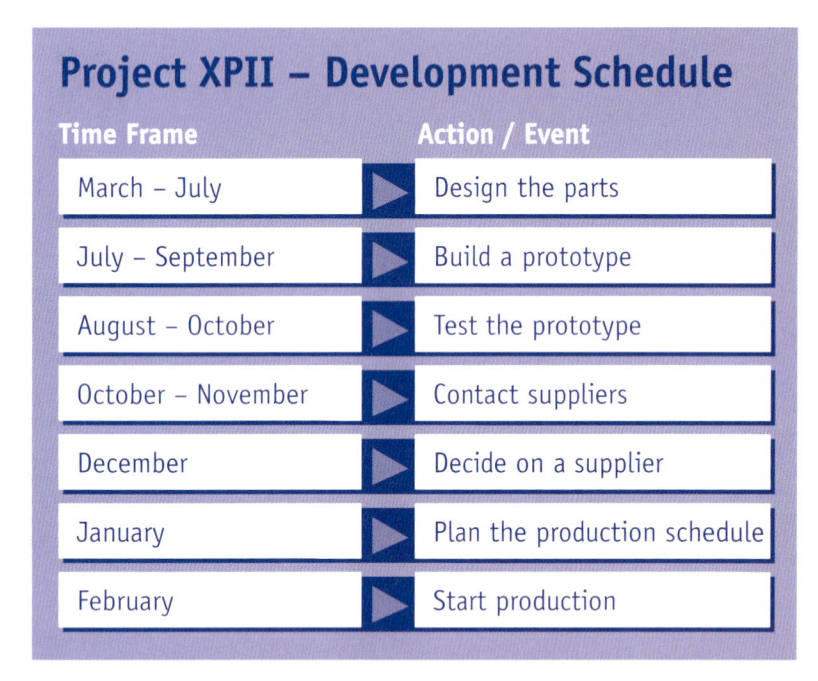

Project XPII – Development Schedule

Time Frame	Action / Event
March – July	Design the parts
July – September	Build a prototype
August – October	Test the prototype
October – November	Contact suppliers
December	Decide on a supplier
January	Plan the production schedule
February	Start production

2 Listen to student B's description and complete the chart. Remember to confirm that you understand.

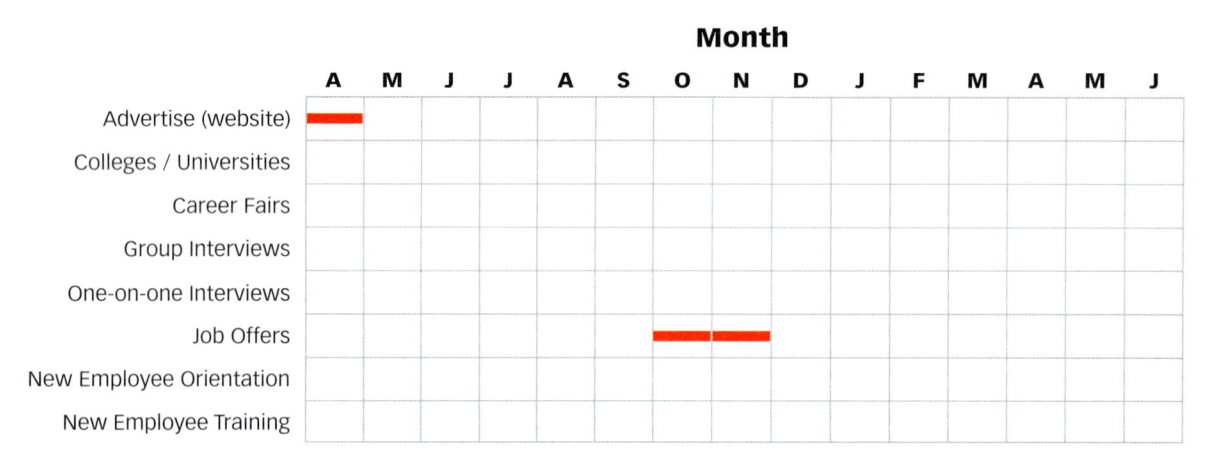

Month

	A	M	J	J	A	S	O	N	D	J	F	M	A	M	J
Advertise (website)	■	■													
Colleges / Universities															
Career Fairs															
Group Interviews															
One-on-one Interviews															
Job Offers							■	■							
New Employee Orientation															
New Employee Training															

3 Compare your books. Did you get the correct information?

UNIT 11 Get Ready for International Business

Talk business

Student A: use this page Student B: use page 107

Useful language

A: Would you like a / some (___)?	B: Sure. Where is it / are they from?
A: It's / They're from (___).	B: What's in it / them?
A: (___).	B: Thank you. It looks / They look delicious.

1 Offer student B these dishes. Answer B's questions.

a summer rolls

b gravlax

c harira

summer rolls, Vietnam
rice noodles, shrimp, vegetables

gravlax, Norway
salmon (fish), salt and sugar, mustard

harira, Morocco
lamb, tomatoes, beans, spices

2 Student B will offer you these dishes. Ask where they are from and what is in them. Then accept the offer.

d shepherd's pie

e pavlova

f pakoras

Talk business **UNIT 12** **95**

Talk business

Student B: use this page Student A: use page 84

Useful language

What	do	you	do?
Who	are do	you	with work for?
What	is	your	address? postcode? phone number? email address?

1 Answer student A's questions about your business card.

Chris Chandler
production assistant

Northwest Media Services
We produce top-quality videos

66 Eccles Street
Dublin 7
(01) 4840703
c_chand@nwmedia.net

2 Ask questions to complete student A's business card below. Write A's responses.

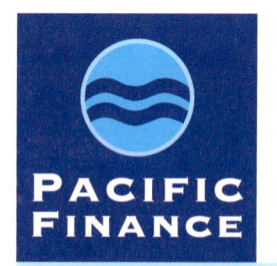

PACIFIC FINANCE

Mary Chan
_____

Personal Banking _____

105 Thomson Road ... Tel: 6355 5749
_____ United Square ... Fax: 6355 _____
Singapore _____
email: _____ @ _____

3 Compare your books. Did you get the correct information?

UNIT 1 Get Ready for International Business

Talk business

Student B: use this page Student A: use page 85

Useful language

Do you	write emails? take part in one-on-one meetings? take part in teleconferences?
How often do you	give presentations? make telephone calls? go on overseas business trips?

1 Answer student A's questions. Use this information.

Asia Research Centre – Survey of on-the-job use of English

Activity	Yes / No	How often?
read emails	Yes	every day
write emails	Yes	once a week
take part in one-on-one meetings	No	–
take part in group meetings	Yes	once a month
use the telephone	No	–
take part in teleconferences	No	–
give presentations	Yes	every month
go on overseas business trips	Yes	twice a year
other: *welcome foreign visitors*	Yes	three or four times a year

2 Ask student A questions to complete the survey about A's on-the-job use of English. Write A's responses.

Asia Research Centre – Survey of on-the-job use of English

Activity	Yes / No	How often?
read emails		
write emails		
take part in one-on-one meetings		
take part in group meetings		
use the telephone		
take part in teleconferences		
give presentations		
go on overseas business trips		
other: *give factory tours*		

3 Compare your books. Did you get the correct information?

Talk business

Student B: use this page Student A: use page 86

Useful language

What		does	your company	do?
Where		is	your head office?	
When		was	the company	established?
How many	offices / employees	do	you	have?

1 Answer student A's questions about Rock On! Records.

Rock On! Records

Head office:	London, U.K.
Established:	1998
Employees:	214
Offices:	London, New York
Factories:	Tokyo, Zurich
Business:	produces music

2 Ask student A questions to get information about Fujimoto Heavy Industries. Complete the table.

Fujimoto Heavy Industries

Head office:	
Established:	
Employees:	
Offices:	
Factories:	
Business:	

3 Compare your books. Did you get the correct information?

98 UNIT 3 Get Ready for International Business

Talk business

Student B: use this page Student A: use page 87

Useful language

You should …	
Why don't you … ?	That's a good idea, thanks.
I recommend …	Well, maybe.
How about … ?	

1 Listen to student A's problems. Make suggestions using the information below.

shop online
buy a new one
drink some coffee

get up earlier
check a dictionary
get a part-time job

2 Tell student A your problems. Listen to A's suggestions.

If you like the suggestion, say, 'That's a good idea, thanks.'

If you don't like the suggestion, say, 'Well, maybe.'

a I need to buy my friend a gift.
b I can't use my digital camera.
c I don't remember my teacher's name.
d I don't like this shirt.
e I need more exercise.

Talk business

Student B: use this page Student A: use page 88

Useful language

How do you spell (that)?
Can you speak more slowly?
Can you speak more loudly?

Can you repeat that?
Can you say that again?

1 You are the receiver.

You will receive a phone call from student A. You are the receptionist for CNS Marketing. Ms Cho is not at her desk now.

Take a message using the form below. Remember to thank the caller and end the phone call!

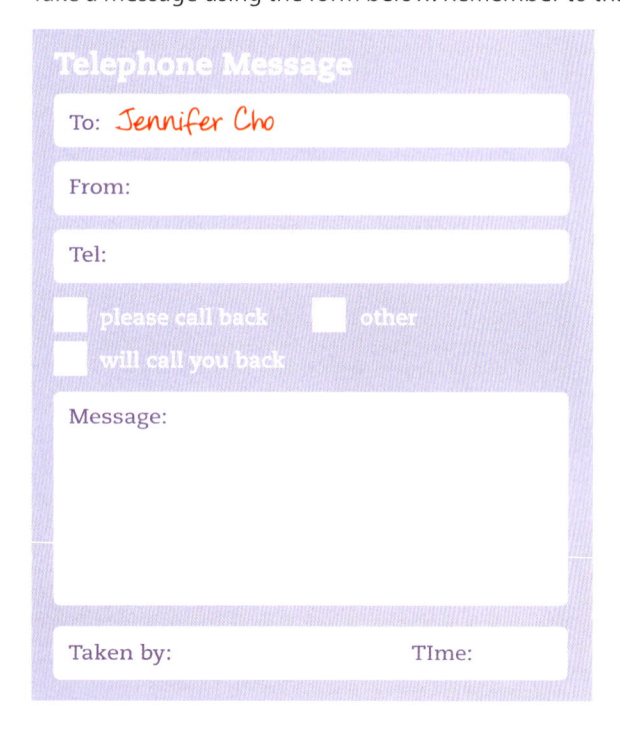

Telephone Message
To: Jennifer Cho
From:
Tel:
☐ please call back   ☐ other
☐ will call you back
Message:
Taken by: TIme:

2 You are the caller.

You are Lisa Gomez at Aztec Coffee.
Your phone number is: 55 – 5286 – 1397.

Call student A and ask for Margaret Thompson. If she is not there, leave a message. Ask her to call you back this afternoon before 5:30.

Begin the call by saying: *'Ring, ring'.*

3 Compare your books. Did you get the correct information?

Talk business

Student B: use this page Student A: use page 89

Practise the conversation below. Then have similar conversations using the information in the charts.

A: Do you know which (camera) is (cheaper)?

B: Well, (the XLR) is ($300). How about the (Ricon 900)?

A: That one is ($500).

B: OK, then (the XLR) is (cheaper). You should get that one.

1 Talk with shopper A about the smartphone, the English book, and the video game. (A starts.)

1 smartphone – light
the Blueberry: 3 grams
the Strawberry: ____ grams

2 English book – short
Great Grammar: 380 pages
Grammar Fun: ____ pages

3 video game – good
Space Battle: 5 stars
Educational Journey: ____ stars

2 Ask shopper A about the suit, the CD, and the ladder.

Begin like this: *Do you know which suit is more expensive?*

4 suit – expensive
the Yugo Moss: $____
the Nolo: $2,500

5 CD – new
Radio Hits: ____ years old
Hot Hip Hop: 2 years old

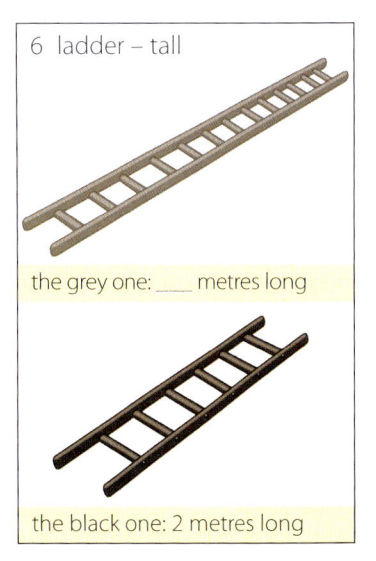

6 ladder – tall
the grey one: ____ metres long
the black one: 2 metres long

3 Compare your books. Did you get the correct information?

Talk business **UNIT 6** 101

Talk business

Student B: use this page Student A: use page 90

Let me confirm.
Let me repeat that.

That's ... .
You said ... .
The ... is ... .

Is that right?

1 Receiver

You are Jenny Sanderson at Pacific Restaurant.

You will receive a phone call. Write down the reservation information in the form. (Remember to check the information!)

Pacific Restaurant **RESERVATION ORDER**

GUEST NAME: _____ DATE: _____ TIME: _____

NO. OF PEOPLE: _____ ADULTS: _____ CHILDREN: _____

TEL: _____

You: Good morning, Pacific Restaurant. How can I help you?
Mary: (Student A)
You: Certainly. Can I have your name, please?
Mary: ....
You: Thank you for your call. We look forward to serving you.

2 Caller

You are Mikel Deuter at Ruhr Pipe.

You are calling Anna Martinez at BL Chemicals. You want to order some parts.

Anna: (Student A)
You: Hello, this is Mikel Deuter at Ruhr Pipe. I'd like to order some parts.
Anna: ...
You: Yes, the first one is ...

This is your order:

Need to order from BL Chemicals:

Part No.	Quantity
DD 3245	877
DK 5666Y	2000
YT4176A	619
YT4177D	1500

3 Compare your books. Did you get the correct information?

Talk business

Student B: use this page Student A: use page 91

Useful language

Where is the _____?
It's …

across from   behind   between   in front of
in the corner   next to / on the left
next to / on the right   under

1 Look at the map of the shopping centre below. Answer student A's questions.

2 Ask student A where these shops are, and write them onto the map: *sweet shop, sportswear shop, Korean restaurant, coffee shop*.

3 Compare your books. Did you get the right information?

Talk business

Student B: use this page   Student A: use page 92

1 Listen to student A's description and complete the first part of the process. Check and confirm that you understand.

Useful language

Yes, that's clear.
I understand.
OK.
I'm with you.

Let me repeat that …
Let me confirm …

Preparing for a job interview.

1 _____ the company

What are _____ _____?
Who are their _____ customers?

2 Plan _____ _____

Where is the office?
_____ _____ does it take to get there?

3 _____

Prepare answers: What are your _____
/ weaknesses / future _____?

4 _____ right

_____ _____ .
Get a haircut.

2 Describe the second part of the process to student A. Check that he / she understands.

Begin like this:
The next step is to arrive early. This means you should be 20 minutes early.

Useful language

Is that clear (so far)?
Are you with me (so far)?
OK?

5 Arrive early

Be 20 minutes early.
Turn off your mobile phone.

6 Don't be shy!

Talk about your experiences.
Show them who you are!

7 Ask questions.

Ask about the company and the job.
Ask about future plans.

8 Follow-up

Next day: Send a thank-you note or email.

3 Compare your books. Did you get the correct information?

Talk business

Student B: use this page   Student A: use page 93

Here is information about visitors to the Grand Canyon in Arizona, US.

1 Answer student A's questions with this information:

a   Most visitors to Grand Canyon National Park, 83 percent, were from the United States. 17 percent of visitors were international.

b

Country	Number of visitors
United Kingdom	227
Canada	209
Japan	129
Germany	117
The Netherlands	71
Australia	65

2   a   Complete the pie chart. Ask student A for information like this:

What percentage of people were (…)?

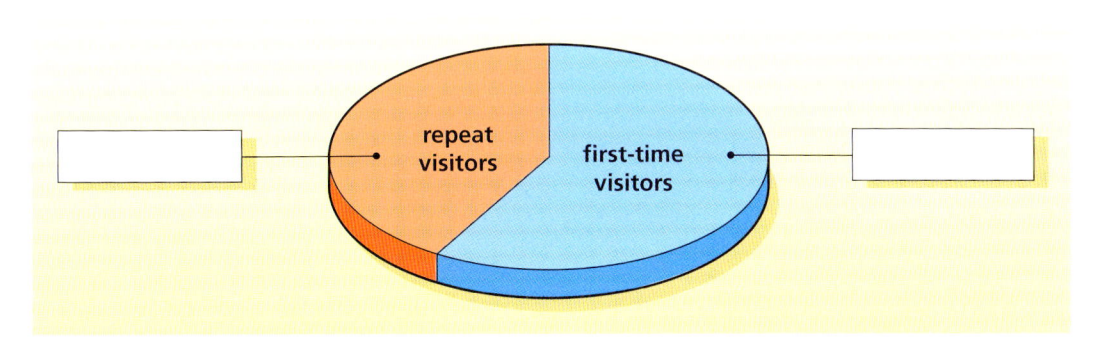

b   Complete the bar graph by drawing in the correct bars for each state. Ask student A for information like this:

How many people came from (…)?

(Bar graph: y-axis 180–740 in increments of 80; x-axis: California, Arizona, Texas, Florida, New York, Ohio)

3   Compare your books. Did you get the correct information?

Talk business

Student B: use this page Student A: use page 94

Useful language

From January to February we In March we	will … are going to … plan to … hope to …

1 Listen to student A's description and complete the chart. Remember to confirm that you understand.

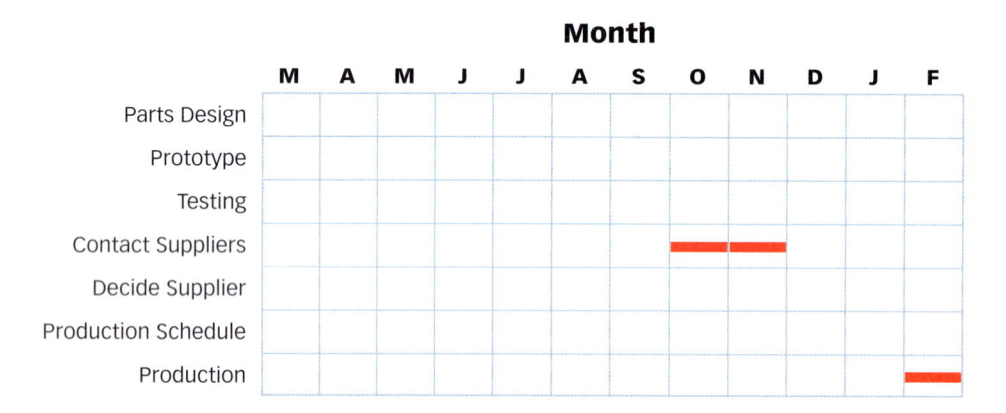

Month

	M	A	M	J	J	A	S	O	N	D	J	F
Parts Design												
Prototype												
Testing												
Contact Suppliers								━	━			
Decide Supplier												
Production Schedule												
Production												━

2 Describe the recruiting timeline to student A. Check that he / she understands.

New Employee Recruitment – Timeline

Time Frame	Action / Event
April	▶ Post job openings on the website
May – June	▶ Visit colleges & universities
July	▶ Attend career fairs
July – August	▶ Interview candidates (group)
August – September	▶ Interview candidates (one-on-one)
October – November	▶ Make job offers
April	▶ Give orientation to new employees
April – June	▶ New employee training

3 Compare your books. Did you get the correct information?

UNIT 11 Get Ready for International Business

Talk business

Student B: use this page Student A: use page 95

Useful language

A: Would you like a / some (____)?	B: Sure. Where is it / are they from?
A: It's / They're from (____).	B: What's in it / them?
A: (____).	B: Thank you. It looks / They look delicious.

1 Student A will offer you these dishes. Ask where they are from and what is in them. Then accept the offer.

a summer rolls

b gravlax

c harira

2 Offer student A these dishes. Answer A's questions.

d shepherd's pie

e pavlova

f pakoras

shepherd's pie, England
beef or lamb, vegetables covered with mashed potatoes

pavlova, Australia
eggs, vanilla, and a lot of sugar!

pakoras, Pakistan
potatoes, onions, flour fried in oil

UNIT 1 TOEIC® practice

LISTENING:

A Photographs

🔊 2.29 Listen. Then choose the sentence that best describes the photo.

1 (A) (B) (C) (D)

2 (A) (B) (C) (D)

B Sentence – Response

🔊 2.30 Listen. Then choose the best response to the sentence you hear.

3 (A) (B) (C)   5 (A) (B) (C)
4 (A) (B) (C)   6 (A) (B) (C)

READING Sentence completion

Choose the best word to complete each sentence.

7 I'm sorry, I didn't _____ your name.
   (A) meet
   (B) know
   (C) give
   (D) catch

8 Well, I'll see you _____ .
   (A) with
   (B) later
   (C) after
   (D) ahead

9 What's the country _____ for Germany?
   (A) code
   (B) hyphen
   (C) area
   (D) city

10 I'm a Sales _____ .
    (A) Marketing
    (B) Developer
    (C) Product
    (D) Representative

11 I'm _____ Purchasing.
    (A) at
    (B) for
    (C) in
    (D) on

12 _____ me give you my card.
    (A) Tell
    (B) Let
    (C) See
    (D) Hear

108 UNIT 1 Get Ready for International Business

UNIT 2 TOEIC® practice

LISTENING: Short conversations and talks

2.31 Listen. Then answer the questions.

1. Who are the speakers?
   (A) Strangers meeting each other
   (B) A clerk and a customer
   (C) Business co-workers
   (D) Husband and wife

2. What are they planning to do?
   (A) Type an order
   (B) Attend a meeting
   (C) Make a phone call
   (D) Buy a product

3. Where are the speakers?
   (A) At a restaurant
   (B) At work
   (C) At the airport
   (D) At a train station

4. What is the woman asking about?
   (A) A schedule
   (B) A map
   (C) A phone call
   (D) A watch

5. What is the man talking about?
   (A) His company's working hours
   (B) His new job schedule
   (C) His daily routine
   (D) His boss's business trip

6. What time does the meeting start?
   (A) 7:00
   (B) 7:30
   (C) 8:00
   (D) 8:30

READING: Passage completion

Read the passage. Choose the best word to complete each sentence.

From: oliv67@dfsinternet.co.uk **To:** anyab@yahoo.com **Subject:** New job!

Hi Anya,

I started my new job this week. I really like it. I have to get up early, because it starts _____ 7:30 in the morning! I _____ for coffee and a muffin most days because I don't

7. (A) in
   (B) at
   (C) on
   (D) to

8. (A) stop
   (B) try
   (C) eat
   (D) make

have time to eat at home. We usually _____ a short morning meeting, and then there's a

9. (A) has
   (B) have
   (C) having
   (D) are having

long meeting _____ a week on Fridays. I don't have much work yet because I just

10. (A) every
    (B) some
    (C) twice
    (D) once

started, but I'm sure I'll really like it. I'll email you next week.

See you,

Olivia

UNIT 3 TOEIC® practice

LISTENING:
A Photographs

🔊 **2.32** Listen. Then choose the sentence that best describes the photo.

1   (A) (B) (C) (D)

2   (A) (B) (C) (D)

B Sentence – Response

🔊 **2.33** Listen. Then choose the best response to the sentence you hear.

3   (A) (B) (C)   5   (A) (B) (C)
4   (A) (B) (C)   6   (A) (B) (C)

READING Sentence completion

Choose the best word to complete each sentence.

7   Our office has 125 _____ employees.
   (A) head
   (B) full-time
   (C) worker
   (D) developed

8   Our company _____ in 2004.
   (A) is established
   (B) established
   (C) was established
   (D) were established

9   We have seven factories _____ other countries.
   (A) in
   (B) at
   (C) on
   (D) with

10 This company _____ chemical products.
   (A) sale
   (B) sales
   (C) sell
   (D) sells

11 Can you _____ your telephone number?
   (A) repeat
   (B) do
   (C) make
   (D) ask

12 I _____ work for a small company.
   (A) was wanted
   (B) want
   (C) want to
   (D) am wanting

UNIT 4 TOEIC® practice

LISTENING: Short conversations and talks

🔊 2.34 Listen. Then answer the questions.

1. What does the man think about the woman?
   (A) She looks angry.
   (B) She has good manners.
   (C) She is tired.
   (D) She doesn't work hard.

2. What does the man recommend?
   (A) A vacation
   (B) A shorter schedule
   (C) More training
   (D) A new job

3. What is the woman probably going to do?
   (A) Help her boss with his work
   (B) Go see her manager
   (C) Work on the weekend
   (D) Ask for a day off

4. What is the woman talking about?
   (A) Working overtime
   (B) A company party
   (C) Her personal life
   (D) Her coworkers

5. What time does the event start?
   (A) 6:00am
   (B) 9:00am
   (C) 6:00pm
   (D) 9:00pm

6. What does the woman say about food?
   (A) People will pay for their own food.
   (B) They will eat cafeteria food.
   (C) There won't be any food.
   (D) People should recommend food to her.

READING: Reading comprehension

Read the letter. Then answer the questions.

Dear Ms Morales,

It is my pleasure to write this letter for Victor Hart. I have known Victor for three years. He was my English student last year, and he worked on the student newspaper with me for three years.

    Victor is bright and hard-working. He enjoys challenging subjects and doesn't get frustrated with difficult tasks. His academic work is excellent, and he gets along well with his classmates and has many friends.

    Finally, Victor worked this year as an assistant in the front office. He answered phone calls, typed letters, and helped with general office work. Everyone was pleased with his good work.

    I think Victor would be an excellent student for your university program. Please contact me by phone or email if you have any further questions.

Sincerely,

Matthew J. Lauer

Matthew J. Lauer
English Department
Thomas Jefferson High School

7. What is the purpose of this letter?
   (A) To ask some questions
   (B) To say thank you
   (C) To discuss a problem
   (D) To make a recommendation

8. Who is Matthew J. Lauer?
   (A) A high school student
   (B) A university student
   (C) A high school teacher
   (D) A university professor

9. What does the letter NOT say about Victor?
   (A) He has worked in an office.
   (B) He likes challenging work.
   (C) He wants to study English.
   (D) He is a friendly person.

10. What does Victor want to do?
    (A) Go to a university
    (B) Get a job in an office
    (C) Take a high school class
    (D) Work for a newspaper

UNIT 5 TOEIC® practice

LISTENING:
A Photographs

2.35 Listen. Then choose the sentence that best describes the photo.

1 (A) (B) (C) (D)   2 (A) (B) (C) (D)

B Sentence – Response

2.36 Listen. Then choose the best response to the sentence you hear.

3 (A) (B) (C)   5 (A) (B) (C)
4 (A) (B) (C)   6 (A) (B) (C)

READING Sentence completion

Choose the best word to complete each sentence.

7 I _____ him your message.
   (A) give
   (B) will give
   (C) am giving
   (D) giving

8 I'm sorry, I can't _____ you.
   (A) listen
   (B) speak
   (C) talk
   (D) hear

9 Just a moment. I'll _____ your call.
   (A) transfer
   (B) exchange
   (C) change
   (D) repeat

10 Can you speak more _____ ?
   (A) slow
   (B) slower
   (C) slowly
   (D) slowing

11 Ms Creswell is on another _____ .
   (A) message
   (B) line
   (C) desk
   (D) vacation

12 Can you say that _____ ?
   (A) another
   (B) again
   (C) later
   (D) out

UNIT 6 TOEIC® practice

LISTENING: Short conversations and talks

2.37 Listen. Then answer the questions.

1 What are the people talking about?
 (A) A printer
 (B) A watch
 (C) A laptop
 (D) A cell phone

2 Why does the woman like it?
 (A) It's not very expensive.
 (B) She has a coupon for it.
 (C) It's very reliable.
 (D) She wants a large one.

3 What does the man suggest?
 (A) Buying a different one
 (B) Asking for a discount
 (C) Getting a different colour
 (D) Buying it later

4 Where could you hear this announcement?
 (A) In a store
 (B) On the radio
 (C) On the phone
 (D) In an office

5 What is the man talking about?
 (A) A sale
 (B) A new model
 (C) A store
 (D) A special service

6 What can you get with the EZ-500?
 (A) A 20% discount
 (B) Free batteries
 (C) A money-back guarantee
 (D) Free shipping

READING: Passage completion

Read the passage. Choose the best word to complete each sentence.

T-shirts, jackets, jeans, shoes, and more, all at great prices!

This **week's specials:**
100% _____ men's dress shirts. Buy one, get one _____ !

7 (A) long
 (B) strong
 (C) cotton
 (D) cheap

8 (A) now
 (B) new
 (C) easy
 (D) free

We guarantee that we have _____ prices than any other store in town.

9 (A) better
 (B) good
 (C) more good
 (D) more better

If you're not satisfied, just bring the clothing back for a full _____ .

10 (A) refund
 (B) coupon
 (C) sale
 (D) discount

If you want nicer, _____ clothing, then hurry down to one of our stores.

11 (A) attractive
 (B) more attractive
 (C) kind of attractive
 (D) not so attractive

Or order _____ by visiting our website: http://www.fashionwarehouse.com.

12 (A) on sale
 (B) rather
 (C) actually
 (D) online

UNIT 7 TOEIC® practice

LISTENING:

A Photographs

🔊 2.38 Listen. Then choose the sentence that best describes the photo.

1 (A) (B) (C) (D)

2 (A) (B) (C) (D)

B Sentence – Response

🔊 2.39 Listen. Then choose the best response to the sentence you hear.

3 (A) (B) (C) 5 (A) (B) (C)
4 (A) (B) (C) 6 (A) (B) (C)

READING Sentence completion

Choose the best word to complete each sentence.

7 I'm free _____ the afternoon.
(A) by
(B) on
(C) at
(D) in

8 I'm calling to _____ my reservation.
(A) confirm
(B) return
(C) order
(D) speak

9 I want to _____ the meeting time.
(A) make
(B) call
(C) change
(D) end

10 Are you free on Tuesday _____ ?
(A) afternoon
(B) the afternoon
(C) early
(D) earlier

11 I'd like _____ a pizza.
(A) order
(B) ordering
(C) to order
(D) ordered

12 Could you ask her to return _____ call?
(A) her
(B) my
(C) him
(D) its

114 UNIT 7 Get Ready for International Business

UNIT 8 TOEIC® practice

LISTENING: Short conversations and talks

2.40 Listen. Then answer the questions.

1. Where are the speakers?
   - (A) In a hotel room
   - (B) At a reception area
   - (C) On a factory floor
   - (D) In a bank

2. What does the man want to do?
   - (A) Make an appointment
   - (B) Find the stairs
   - (C) Leave a message
   - (D) See Ms Di Angelo

3. Where is the room?
   - (A) On the 10th floor
   - (B) Before the stairs
   - (C) Next to the elevator
   - (D) Down the hallway to the right

4. Where would you hear this announcement?
   - (A) On a train
   - (B) In a movie theater
   - (C) In a restaurant
   - (D) At an airport

5. When can you buy something to eat?
   - (A) In the morning
   - (B) In fifteen minutes
   - (C) At 6:00
   - (D) In half an hour

6. What can you do in the lounge?
   - (A) Use the telephone
   - (B) Order a drink
   - (C) Buy some snacks
   - (D) Watch a film

READING: Reading comprehension

Read the email. Then answer the questions.

From: Mary Allred <mary.allred@goglobal.com>
To: Stephen Parelli <sparelli@newbus.org>
Subject: Monday's business meeting

Hi Steve,

I'm glad you can come in on Monday. Let me tell you how to get here.

The easiest way is to take a taxi to the head office. The address is 521 Albert Street. It should take about ten minutes. When you walk into the building, you'll see stairs and a lift on your left. Go up to the 8th floor. When you get out of the lift, turn left. Our secretary's office is the first room on the right. My office is three doors after that, between the copy room and the stairs.

If you get lost or are going to be late, just call my mobile phone.

I look forward to seeing you at 9:30.

Best wishes,
Mary

7. What is the purpose of this email?
   - (A) To make an appointment
   - (B) To give directions
   - (C) To make an introduction
   - (D) To request some help

8. How do Steve Parelli and Mary Allred know each other?
   - (A) They work in the same building.
   - (B) Mary is Steve's secretary.
   - (C) Steve is applying for a job with Mary.
   - (D) They are doing business together.

9. Where is the secretary's office?
   - (A) Next to the stairs
   - (B) On the 12th floor
   - (C) Before Mary's office
   - (D) In front of the lift

10. How can Steve contact Mary if he has a problem?
    - (A) By telephone
    - (B) By talking to her secretary
    - (C) By email
    - (D) In person

UNIT 9 TOEIC® practice

LISTENING:

A Photographs

🔊 2.41 Listen. Then choose the sentence that best describes the photo.

1 (A) (B) (C) (D)

2 (A) (B) (C) (D)

B Sentence – Response

🔊 2.42 Listen. Then choose the best response to the sentence you hear.

3 (A) (B) (C)   5 (A) (B) (C)
4 (A) (B) (C)   6 (A) (B) (C)

READING Sentence completion

Choose the best word to complete each sentence.

7   The first step is _____ customers.
    (A) talk
    (B) talking to
    (C) talked
    (D) to talk

8   _____ the same time, add some water.
    (A) To
    (B) At
    (C) After
    (D) In

9   How long does the process _____?
    (A) be
    (B) plan
    (C) take
    (D) cost

10 Finally, we _____ delivery to our customers.
    (A) arrange
    (B) enter
    (C) send
    (D) order

11 Let me _____ sure I understand.
    (A) check
    (B) see
    (C) make
    (D) know

12 Is that clear _____ far?
    (A) so
    (B) too
    (C) very
    (D) all

UNIT 10 TOEIC® practice

LISTENING: Short conversations and talks

2.43 Listen. Then answer the questions.

1. What does the man want to know?
   (A) The delivery schedule
   (B) What fax machines to order
   (C) How much a product will cost
   (D) The date of a meeting

2. What does the woman offer to do?
   (A) Find some information
   (B) Conduct a training session
   (C) Type a document
   (D) Hire a new worker

3. What does the man say about her offer?
   (A) He wants her to do something different.
   (B) He is pleased about it.
   (C) He says it isn't necessary.
   (D) He doesn't think it will work.

4. What is the speaker doing?
   (A) He's checking some data.
   (B) He's giving a presentation.
   (C) He's developing a plan.
   (D) He's training some employees.

5. In what month were sales the highest?
   (A) September
   (B) October
   (C) November
   (D) December

6. What does the man suggest that people do next?
   (A) Ask any questions they have
   (B) Check some information
   (C) Go home and come back the next day
   (D) Take a short break

READING: Paired reading

Read the chart and letter. Then answer the questions.

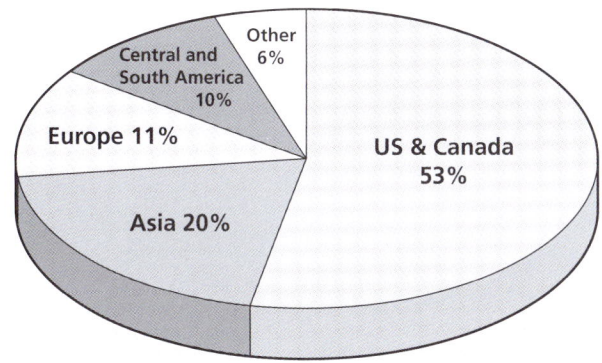

Guests at the Central Plaza Hotel by country of origin, 2013

- US & Canada 53%
- Asia 20%
- Europe 11%
- Central and South America 10%
- Other 6%

Dear Frank,

Thank you for meeting with me on Thursday. I'm enclosing a pie chart of the country of origin of our guests. As you can see, most of our guests are from North America, but recently, guests from Asia have increased sharply, probably because of your great advertising campaign.

Now I'd like to do the same for Europe... the number of guests from Europe has remained about the same for the past few years. I'd like to increase that number in 2014. Let's meet again next Thursday at the same time to talk about this.

Best,

Joanne

7. What does the pie chart show?
   (A) How many guests stayed at the hotel
   (B) How much money the hotel earned
   (C) Where the hotel's guests came from
   (D) Where the hotel branches are located

8. How many guests come from Europe?
   (A) 5%
   (B) 10%
   (C) 11%
   (D) 20%

9. What has increased sharply?
   (A) The hotel's profits from guests
   (B) The percentage of guests from the US and Canada
   (C) The cost of advertising campaigns
   (D) The number of guests from Asia

10. What does Joanne want?
    (A) To get more guests from Europe
    (B) To offer more services at the hotel
    (C) To decrease the number of guests from Asia
    (D) To charge more money for hotel rooms

UNIT 11 TOEIC® practice

LISTENING:

A Photographs

2.44 Listen. Then choose the sentence that best describes the photo.

1 (A) (B) (C) (D)

2 (A) (B) (C) (D)

B Sentence – Response

2.45 Listen. Then choose the best response to the sentence you hear.

3 (A) (B) (C)   5 (A) (B) (C)
4 (A) (B) (C)   6 (A) (B) (C)

READING Sentence completion

Choose the best word to complete each sentence.

7 Please finish the report _____ 6:00.
   (A) on
   (B) from
   (C) by
   (D) until

8 I'll work on this _____ away.
   (A) right
   (B) now
   (C) already
   (D) just

9 What are you going _____ this afternoon?
   (A) do
   (B) doing
   (C) to do
   (D) are doing

10 We're planning to _____ our business.
   (A) meet
   (B) hire
   (C) take
   (D) expand

11 In three years, I'll probably _____ a manager.
   (A) be
   (B) will be
   (C) being
   (D) am

12 I hope to _____ to a different office.
   (A) pack
   (B) transfer
   (C) arrange
   (D) build

UNIT 12 TOEIC® practice

LISTENING: Short conversations and talks

2.46 Listen. Then answer the questions.

1. What does the woman ask about?
   - (A) How to eat enchiladas
   - (B) Where enchiladas come from
   - (C) What enchiladas are made from
   - (D) Who cooked the enchiladas

2. What does the man NOT say is in the enchiladas?
   - (A) A sauce
   - (B) Cheese
   - (C) Vegetables
   - (D) Beans

3. Why won't the woman eat the enchiladas?
   - (A) She's on a diet.
   - (B) She doesn't eat meat.
   - (C) The food doesn't look good.
   - (D) She's already eaten some.

4. At what occasion is the man speaking?
   - (A) A wedding
   - (B) A business meeting
   - (C) A birthday party
   - (D) A family dinner

5. How does the speaker know Joe?
   - (A) He is Joe's brother.
   - (B) He and Joe went to the same school.
   - (C) He hired Joe for a job.
   - (D) He is Joe's manager at work.

6. What is Joe going to do soon?
   - (A) Serve food to his guests
   - (B) Hire more staff at work
   - (C) Open a new office
   - (D) Move to another country

READING: Passage completion

Read the passage. Choose the best word to complete each sentence.

Business Entertaining
Focus on Australia

To be successful on your business trip to Australia, follow these tips for mealtimes:

* Keep your hands above the table when you eat. Australians hold the _____ in the left hand and the knife in the right hand.
   - 7 (A) fork
   - (B) sauce
   - (C) food
   - (D) salad

* If you're invited _____ dinner, come on time. For an informal party, it's OK to be 15 minutes late.
   - 8 (A) in
   - (B) on
   - (C) at
   - (D) to

* It's polite to _____ something to drink or a small gift if you're invited to someone's home.
   - 9 (A) have
   - (B) bring
   - (C) dip
   - (D) put

* Barbecues are _____. Meat is a common _____ served at these outdoor parties.
   - 10 (A) allergic
   - (B) popular
   - (C) clever
   - (D) kind
   - 11 (A) plate
   - (B) dish
   - (C) hand
   - (D) diet

* Australians are friendly and casual at mealtimes. Just relax and enjoy the _____ occasion.
   - 12 (A) socialised
   - (B) socialise
   - (C) society
   - (D) social

* Save business for the office.

Wordlist

(n) = noun (v) = verb (adj) = adjective (adv) = adverb

Unit 1

accountant (n)
administrative assistant (n)
advertising (n)
area code (n)
business card (n)
construction (n)
conversation (n)
country code (n)
department (n)
designer (n)
dot (n)
email (v)
engineer (n)
human resources (n)
imaginary (adj)
information technology (n)
limited (adj)
logo (n)
manager (n)
marketing (n)
meet (v)
planner (n)
post code (n)
pretend (v)
product (n)
purchase (v)
researcher (n)
sales assistant (n)
underscore (v)
zip code (n)

Unit 2

customer (n)
manufacturing (n)
married (adj)
meeting (n)
muffin (n)
pass (n)
presentation (n)
sandwich (n)
schedule (n)
support (n)
teleconference (n)
train (n)

Unit 3

build (v)
design (v)
develop (v)
employee (n)
establish (v)
full-time (adj)
integrated circuit (n)
produce (v)
provide (v)

Unit 4

advice (n)
angry (adj)
boring (adj)
confusing (adj)
corporate (adj)
culture (n)
custom (n)
difficult (adj)
earlier (adj)
exhausted (adj)
frustrating (adj)
hiking (n)
impolite (adj)
manual (n)
miss (v)
online (adj)
paint (v)
polite (adj)
pretty (adv)
situation (n)
sleepy (adj)
small talk (n)
tone (n)
training (n)

Unit 5

finance (n)
message (n)
receptionist (n)
text message (n)
transfer (v)

Unit 6

compact *(adj)*
discount *(n)*
display *(v)*
efficient *(adj)*
energy *(n)*
expensive *(adj)*
fashionable *(adj)*
heavy *(adj)*
ladder *(n)*
light *(adj)*
mailing *(n)*
package *(n)*
smartphone *(n)*
promise *(v)*
quality *(n)*
refreshing *(adj)*
reliable *(adj)*
scooter *(n)*
script *(n)*
shredder *(n)*
smartphone *(n)*
worse *(adj)*

Unit 7

chat *(v)*
complicated *(adj)*
formal *(adj)*
efficient *(adj)*
inefficient *(adj)*
informal *(adj)*
quantity *(n)*
reservation *(n)*
simple *(adj)*

Unit 8

cash machine *(n)*
cosmetics [plural] *(n)*
drinking fountain *(n)*
furniture *(n)*
hall *(n)*
lift *(n)*
personal assistant *(n)*

Unit 9

curriculum vitae (CV) *(n)*
data *(n)*
delivery *(n)*
feedback *(n)*
flow chart *(n)*
inventory *(n)*
invoice *(n)*
launch *(v)*
layout *(n)*
professional *(adj)*
recruit *(v)*
shy *(adj)*
smoothie *(n)*
strength *(n)*
turn off *(phrasal verb)*
weakness *(n)*

Unit 10

audience *(n)*
atmosphere *(n)*
average *(adj)*
bar graph *(n)*
budget *(n)*
complaint *(n)*
decrease *(v)*
distracting *(adj)*
increase *(v)*
invent *(v)*
joke *(v)*
joke *(n)*
official *(adj)*
pie chart *(n)*
population *(n)*
prime minister *(n)*
sharply *(adv)*
slightly *(adv)*
topic *(n)*
visual aid *(n)*

Unit 11

agenda *(n)*
contract *(n)*
cost *(n)*
estimate *(n)*
expand *(v)*
hire *(v)*
marathon *(n)*
next *(adj)*
overseas *(adv)*
send *(v)*
step *(n)*

Unit 12

accessory *(n)*
allergic *(adj)*
brownie *(n)*
chopstick *(n)*
compliment *(n)*
dip *(v)*
impression *(n)*
hurt (someone's feelings) *(v)*
diet *(n)*
recipe *(n)*
salty *(adj)*
shrimp *(n)*
spicy *(adj)*
vanilla *(n)*
vegetarian *(adj)*

Look it Up

These words are all on the Viewpoints pages and the definitions are taken from the *Macmillan English Dictionary* second edition.

All red words have a 'star rating':

★★★ the 2,500 most common and basic English words
★★ very common words
★ fairly common words

Unit 1

fancy (adj) ★
not plain or simple but with a lot of decorations or extra parts

organize (v) ★★★
to put things into a sensible order or into a system in which all parts work well together

plain (adj) ★★
simple in design, with no decoration

pocket (n) ★★★
a small bag that forms part of a piece of clothing and is used for holding small objects

receive (v) ★★★
to get something that someone gives or sends to you

respect (n) ★★★
a feeling that something is important and deserves serious attention

Unit 2

flexitime (n)
a system in which workers choose the hours each day that they work, as long as the hours add up to the same fixed number of hours every week or month
(*American* flextime)

holiday (n) ★★★
the number of days or weeks during a year when you do not have to work but are paid.
(*American* vacation)

overtime (n) ★
extra hours that someone works at their job

property developer (n)
someone who earns money by buying land and building on it

telecommuter (n)
someone who works from home on a computer and sends work to their office over telephone lines by MODEM or FAX

time off (n)
time when you are not at work or at school

Unit 3

automotive (adj)
relating to cars

banking (n) ★★
the work done by banks and other financial institutions

chemical (adj) ★★
involving chemistry or produced by a method used in chemistry

education (n) ★★★
the activity of educating people in schools, colleges, and universities, and all the policies and arrangements concerning this

electronics (n) ★★
the science and technology that uses or produces electronic equipment

entertainment (n) ★★
performances that people enjoy

farming (n) ★
the activity or business of being a farmer

fishing (n) ★★
the sport or business of catching fish

health care (n) ★★
the services that look after people's health

hospitality (n) ★
food, drink, and entertainment given to customers by a company or organization

IT (n) ★
information technology: the use of computers and other electronic equipment to store, process, and send information

the media (n) ★★★
radio, television, newspapers, the internet, and magazines considered as a group: can be followed by a singular or plural verb

mining (n) ★
the process of getting coal or metal from under the ground

news (n) ★★★
information about recent events that is reported in newspapers or on television or radio

pharmaceutical (adj)
relating to the production or sale of medicines and drugs used for treating medical conditions

Extracts from the *Macmillan English Dictionary* second edition published 2007 © Macmillan Publishers Limited 2007.
www.macmillandictionaries.com

Get Ready for International Business

software (n) ★★★
programs used by computers for doing particular jobs

tourism (n) ★★
the business of providing services for people who are travelling for their holiday

transportation (n) ★
the activity of moving people or things from one place to another, or the system used for doing this

Unit 4

casual (adj) ★★
relaxed and informal

greet (v) ★★
to behave in a polite or friendly way towards someone when you meet them

manners [plural] (n) ★★★
traditionally accepted ways of behaving that show a polite respect for other people

opinion (n) ★★★
the attitude that you have towards something, especially your thoughts about how good it is

praise (v) ★★
to express strong approval or admiration for someone or something, especially in public

Unit 5

alarm (n) ★★
(an alarm clock: a clock that wakes you up at a particular time by making a noise)

convenient (adj) ★★
easy to do, or not causing problems or difficulties

text (v)
to send a written message to someone using a mobile phone
(*American* **cell phone**)

text message (n)
A written message that you send or receive using a mobile phone

Unit 6

annoyed (adj) ★★
feeling slightly angry or impatient

bother (v) ★★★
if you do not bother to do something, you do not do it, either because there seems to be no good reason or because it involves too much effort

celebrity (n) ★
a famous person, especially in entertainment or sport

competitor (n) ★★
a company that sells the same goods or services as another company

endorsement (n)
an occasion when someone famous says in an advertisement that they like a product

especially (adv) ★★★
used when mentioning conditions that make something more relevant, important, or true

flash (v) ★★
to shine brightly for a very short time, or to shine on and off very quickly

image (n) ★★★
a photograph, painting, or other work of art that represents a person or thing

interrupt (v) ★★
to make something stop for a period of time

Unit 7

chat (v) ★★
to exchange messages with someone using a computer so that you are able to see each other's messages immediately, especially on the internet

complicated (adj) ★★
difficult to do, deal with, or understand, especially because of involving a lot of different processes or aspects

formal (adj) ★★★
following the correct or suitable official methods

efficient (adj) ★★★
something that is efficient works well and produces good results by using the available time, money, supplies etc in the most effective way

inefficient (adj)
not working in the best possible way, especially by not using time, supplies, energy etc in the most effective way

informal (adj) ★★
relaxed and friendly

simple (adj) ★★★
easy to understand, solve, or do

teleconference (n)
a meeting held among people in different places using an electronic communications system, often television

Unit 8

chemist (n) ★★
a shop that sells medicines, beauty products and toiletries

clinic (n) ★★
a place where people go to receive a particular type of medical treatment or advice

convenience store (n)
a small shop that is open for long hours and sells a variety of goods, especially food and drink, cleaning materials, and newspapers or magazines

facility (n) ★★★
something such as a room or piece of equipment that is provided at a place for people to use

flexible (adj) ★★
able to make changes or deal with a situation that is changing

Extracts from the *Macmillan English Dictionary* second edition published 2007 © Macmillan Publishers Limited 2007.
www.macmillandictionaries.com

Look it Up

insurance *(n)* ★★★
an arrangement in which you regularly pay an **insurance company** an amount of money so that they will give you money if something you own is damaged, lost, or stolen, or if you die or are ill or injured

laundry *(n)* ★
a business that washes and irons clothes

shift *(n)* ★★
a period of work time in a factory, hospital, or other place where some people work during the day and some work at night

vending machine *(n)*
a machine that you can buy things from, for example cigarettes, sweets, or drinks
(*American* candy)

yoga *(n)*
an activity that involves doing physical and breathing exercises to make you stronger and make your mind and body relax

Unit 9

graduate *(v)* ★
to complete your studies at a university or college, usually by getting a **degree**

internship *(n)*
a job that a student or someone who has recently obtained a degree takes in order to get experience

recommend *(v)* ★★★
to say that someone or something is good and worth using, having, or experiencing

Unit 10

slide *(n)* ★★
a small piece of film in a frame, that you shine light through in order to show the image on a screen

Unit 11

continue *(v)* ★★★
to keep doing something without stopping

Unit 12

appreciate *(v)* ★★
to recognize the good or special qualities of a person, place, or thing

communal *(adj)* ★
owned or used by everyone in a group, especially a group of people who live in the same building

entertain *(v)* ★★
to receive someone as a guest and give them food and drink or other forms of enjoyment

left-handed *(adj)*
someone who is left-handed is born with a natural tendency to use their left hand to do things, especially things such as writing

social *(adj)* ★★★
relating to activities that involve being with other people, especially activities that you do for pleasure

traditional *(adj)* ★★★
relating to or based on very old customs, beliefs, or stories

Extracts from the *Macmillan English Dictionary* second edition published 2007 © Macmillan Publishers Limited 2007.
www.macmillandictionaries.com

Common irregular verbs

Here is a list of common irregular verbs in English with their past tense (*I **took** the test*) and past participle (*I have **taken** three tests this month*).

Base form	Simple past	Past participle
be	was/were	been
become	became	become
begin	began	begun
break	broke	broken
bring	brought	brought
buy	bought	bought
catch	caught	caught
choose	chose	chosen
come	came	come
cost	cost	cost
cut	cut	cut
do	did	done
draw	drew	drawn
drink	drank	drunk
drive	drove	driven
eat	ate	eaten
fall	fell	fallen
feel	felt	felt
find	found	found
fly	flew	flown
forget	forgot	forgotten
get	got	got
give	gave	given
go	went	gone
have	had	had
hear	heard	heard
know	knew	known
leave	left	left
lose	lost	lost
make	made	made
meet	met	met
pay	paid	paid
put	put	put
read	read	read
ride	rode	ridden
run	ran	run
say	said	said
see	saw	seen
sell	sold	sold
send	sent	sent
show	showed	shown
sing	sang	sung
sit	sat	sat
sleep	slept	slept
speak	spoke	spoken
spend	spent	spent
stand	stood	stood
swim	swam	swum
take	took	taken
teach	taught	taught
tell	told	told
think	thought	thought
throw	threw	thrown
understand	understood	understood
wear	wore	worn
win	won	won
write	wrote	written

UNIT 1 Grammar reference

The verb *to be*

Use the verb *to be* to give your name, your job, and say what company you're with. Contractions are more common in speech.

Long form	Contractions
I am with Globaltech.	I'm with Globaltech.
I am not with Eurofund.	I'm not with Eurofund.
You / we / they are in Advertising.	You're / we're / they're in Advertising.
You / we / they are not in Sales.	You're / we're / they're not in Sales.
	You / we / they aren't in Sales.
He / she is a Marketing Assistant.	He's / she's a Marketing Assistant.
He / she is not a Manager.	He's / she's not a Manager.
	He / she isn't a Manager.

The present simple — statements

Use the present simple to talk about facts and habits.

Subject	Regular verbs
I / you / we / they	work, live, start, give, leave meet, like, make
He / she / it	works, lives, starts, gives, leaves, meets, likes, makes

I work for IWT.
She gives her business card to lots of people.
My train leaves in an hour.

Practice the verb *to be*

1 Complete the paragraph with words from the box. One word is not used.

aren't	m	re
is	m not	s
isn't		

Nice to meet you. 1) I'_____ Shelly Silver. I work for Immedia. 2) We'_____ a global technology company. 3) I usually work at the head office – that'_____ in Munich. 4) I'_____ there now because I'm in Moscow for three weeks to visit our branch office. 5) Here _____ my card. If you want to meet later, please get in touch. 6) But my mobile phone _____ working here, so please use my email.

2 Write the correct form of *to be*.

1 Mr Kahn _____ from Germany. He's from Austria.
2 A: _____ you Canadian?
   B: Yes, I am.
3 A: _____ this your business card?
   B: No, it _____ .
4 My coworkers and I _____ late today.
5 _____ she new here?
6 I _____ with Lake & Bowen.
7 A: Sorry, am I late?
   B: No, you _____ .
8 I'm looking for Maria and Carlo, but they _____ here.

Practice the present simple – statements

3 Answer the questions.

1 Do you live in Zurich? *No I live in Stuttgart.*
2 Who do you work for?
3 Where do you live?
4 What does your company make?
5 Who do you give your business cards to?

UNIT 2 Grammar reference

Prepositions of time at/on/in

Use **at** with the time of day, with some expressions for part of the day and with special times of the year.

at	2 o'clock, 11:30, half past 6, midnight lunchtime, night Hanukkah, Easter, Eid ul-Fitr

Use **on** with dates, with days of the week and with special holidays. Note, we write '15th May' but we say 'the 15th of May'.

on	15th May, Tuesday, Monday afternoon Mother's Day, New Year's Eve

Use **in** with months, years, seasons and parts of the day

in	July, November, 1955, 2014 winter, autumn, spring the afternoon, the evening

Do not use **at/on/in** with **next/last/every**.

I have a job interview next Tuesday.
We visited China last December.
I go to the gym every evening.

Practice prepositions of time – at/on/in

1 Complete the sentences with *at*, *on* or *in*.

1 _____ March Hiro Makino went to the US. He left Shanghai _____ 15th March and he arrived in New York _____ 7:00pm.

2 In Japan, new employees usually join their companies _____ spring.

3 The meeting is _____ Thursday _____ half past 4. _____ the evening there will be a welcome party.

4 Michel DuBois was born _____ Christmas Day, 1989.

2 Danielle is telling her mother about her week. Complete the description by using *at*, *on*, *in* or *nothing* (–).

'Hi Mum, how was your week? _____ last week I was so busy! I know I say that _____ every week, but this time it's true! _____ Monday I had to work late, I finished _____ 11:00pm and had to take a taxi home. I know, we're always busy _____ autumn, but my boss says that _____ next year we'll employ some more staff, so I hope I can take a holiday _____ June. Anyway, _____ next weekend I'll come home so I'll see you _____ Friday night – the train leaves here _____ 7 o'clock and I'll arrive there _____ 10 _____ the evening. Can you pick me up at the station?'

UNIT 3 Grammar reference

Questions and answers with *do* and *does*

Yes/no questions

Questions that can be answered with *yes* or *no* are formed by putting *do* or *does* before the subject and the main verb.

Statement	Question
I / you / we / they work for a design company.	Do I / you / we / they work for a design company?
He / she lives in Budapest.	Does he / she live in Budapest?

Note: questions can be answered with short answers (*Yes, I do.*; *No, he doesn't.*), but also with additional information (Q: *Does this bus run in the morning?* A: *There's one at 9:00.*).

Information questions *(what, where, when, why, how, how much/often)*

Form information questions with the question word first, then *do* or *does*, and then the subject and main verb.

How many employees do you have?
Where do we eat lunch?
What company does he work for?
How often does she work late?

Practice: questions and answers with *do* and *does*

1 Write the words in the correct order to make questions.

1 do / offices / you / how / have / many ?

2 export / does / goods / your company ?

3 your / you / job / like / do ?

4 to work / in / your friend / does / Tourism / want ?

5 do / does / what / company / your ?

6 time / you / what / work / do / finish ?

2 Match the questions in Practice 1 to the answers a–g. There is one extra answer.

a We design posters and brochures. _____
b Yes, I love it. _____
c Three – two in Germany and one in France. _____
d Usually around six. _____
e We have around 2,300 employees. _____
f Not really. He's looking for a job in Sales. _____
g No, we don't. We only import them. _____

UNIT 4 Grammar reference

Short responses – Me too / So do I / Really? / Neither can I

Use short responses to show agreement or disagreement, to show similar experiences or feelings and to keep the conversation going. The form of the auxiliary verb should match the statement it refers to.

I **love** Chinese food.	So **do** I.	I **don't**.
I'**m** angry with my boss.	So **am** I.	I'**m** not.
I **watched** TV last night.	So **did** I.	I **didn't**.
My boss **was** late to work today.	So **was** I.	I **wasn't**.
My sister **can** play the violin.	So **can** I.	I **can't**.

Where the main statement is negative, use *neither* in place of *so*.

I **can't** use this new software.	Neither **can** I.	I **can**.
I **don't** like long meetings.	Neither **do** I.	I **do**.
I'**ve** never seen Star Wars.	Neither **have** I.	I **have**.

Should (Why don't you...?) and recommend (How about...?)

Use *should, why don't you, recommend* or *how about* to give advice or make a suggestion. Use the base form with *should* and *why don't you*. Use the present participle (*-ing*) with *recommend* and *how about*.

| You should join a gym. | I recommend asking for a raise. |
| Why don't you join a gym? | How about asking for a raise? |

Practice: short responses – Me too / So do I / Really? / Neither can I

1 Respond to Tina's statements with information about yourself.

Tina	You
1 'I don't have his phone number.'	'Don't you?' _____
2 'I have a bad cold.'	'Do you?' _____
3 'I worked hard this morning.'	'Did you?' _____
4 'I've never been to the US.'	'Haven't you?' _____
5 'I can't play mahjong.'	'Can't you?' _____

Practice: Should (Why don't you...?) and recommend (How about...?)

2 Write some advice to your friend.

1 You talk too fast. _____
2 Your hair is too long. _____
3 You look tired. _____
4 You look hungry. _____

UNIT 5 Grammar reference

Can for permission and requests

Use *can* to request information or ask for permission to do something.

Note: Some people use *may* in more formal situations.

Can (May) I speak to Mr Smith? / Can (May) I open the window?

Use *can* to politely ask someone to do something.

Note: We don't use *may* in these situations.

Can you sit here, please? / Can you say that again?

Do not confuse these situations with using *can* for ability:

Can you speak Polish?

Practice: *can* for permission and requests

1 Circle the appropriate response.

1 Can you say your name again, please?
   a Yes, I can.
   b Geeta Singh.
2 Can I speak to the Manager?
   a I'm sorry, he's not here right now.
   b Certainly. Please tell him I called.
3 Can I take a message?
   a No, thank you.
   b No, you can't.
4 Can you use this software?
   a I'm on a business trip.
   b Yes, I can.
5 Can I see you on Tuesday?
   a I'll transfer your call.
   b I'm sorry, I'm busy then.

2 Match the situations 1–5 to the appropriate questions a–e.

1 The person you are speaking to is speaking very fast. _____
2 You want to tell Ms Anton something, but she's not there. _____
3 You don't know who is on the phone. _____
4 You don't know how to write someone's name. _____
5 Someone wants to tell your Manager something, but he's not here. _____

a Can I leave a message?
b Can I take a message?
c Can you spell that for me, please?
d I'm sorry, can you speak more slowly?
e Can I ask who's calling?

UNIT 6 Grammar reference

Comparatives – *faster, more reliable*

Use these basic rules to form comparative adjectives.

Short words (one syllable)	add -*er* or -*r*	old = old**er**, safe = safe**r**
Short words with consonant-vowel-consonant	double the final consonant and add -*er*	big = big**ger**, thin = thin**ner**
Longer words (two syllables) ending in -*y*	drop the -*y* and add -*ier*	easy = eas**ier**
Longer words (two or more syllables)	use **more**	challenging = **more** challenging

Note: some adjectives have irregular comparative forms.
good = better   bad = worse   fun = more fun   far = further

Practice: comparatives – *faster, more reliable*

1 Make sentences comparing these items. Use the comparative form of the adjectives in brackets.

1 fruit / fried chicken (healthy)
  Fruit is healthier than fried chicken.

2 walking / driving (cheap)
  _____

3 hotels / camping (expensive)
  _____

4 LEDs / regular light bulbs (efficient)
  _____

5 bungee jumping / reading a book (exciting)
  _____

2 Complete Luka's presentation to his customers. Use the correct form of the adjectives in brackets.

'Welcome to our new factory! This facility is _____ (big), _____ (modern) and _____ (energy-efficient) than our other factories. This means we can make products here _____ (fast) and _____ (cheap) than before, and with _____ (good) quality. As a result, we can offer our customers _____ (short) delivery times and _____ (few) defects. Let me also say that our workers are _____ (happy) here – the work is _____ (safe), working hours are _____ (short) and the food in the cafeteria is _____ (delicious)! Now, if you come with me ...'

UNIT 7 Grammar reference

Prepositions – *to* and *about*

Prepositional phrases add more information to a sentence. Use *to* for people and *about* for things.

*Can I speak **to** the manager? / I'm calling **about** my appointment.*

Infinitives

We can use infinitives (*to* + verb) to express purpose. They are often used directly after verbs. Always keep the verb part of the infinitive phrase in the base form.

*I'm calling **to ask** about our meeting.*
*I'd like **to confirm** the dates.*

Practice: prepositions – *to* and *about*

1 Complete the dialogue with *to* or *about*.

Mr Williams: Hi, can I speak 1) _____ Mr Al Zaidi, please?
Ms Buchieri: Yes, I'll transfer you. Who am I speaking 2) _____?
Mr Williams: Oh, sorry, this is Mr Williams, from Sanyou.
Ms Buchieri: Thank you, Mr Williams. And what is this 3) _____?
Mr Williams: I'm calling 4) _____ the conference next week.
Ms Buchieri: OK, I'll transfer your call … I'm sorry, he's not answering his phone. Would you like to speak 5) _____ his assistant?
Mr Williams: Yes, that's fine. I'm sure she knows 6) _____ the schedule.

Practice: infinitives

2 Complete the sentences with to and one of the words in the box. There is one extra word.

| ask | check | listen | make |
| meet | order | return | |

1 I'm trying _____ my email, but it won't open.
2 We'd like _____ coffee and tea for about 240 people.
3 Hi, I'd like _____ a reservation for two for Friday at 6:00.
4 I'm calling _____ if we can meet this week.
5 I need _____ Mr Singh's call.
6 He wants _____ me on Wednesday for a job interview.

UNIT 8 Grammar reference

Imperatives

Use the imperative form for orders, instructions, warnings and suggestions. Depending on the situation and on the intonation and stress, the form can be friendly, angry or neutral. The negative form is usually formed with *Don't (Do not)*.

Warnings	Look out!	Don't touch!
Orders	Follow me.	Come here.
Instructions	Turn left at the corner.	Stay inside the yellow lines.
Suggestions	Don't forget to lock your door.	Try the cafeteria. It's great.

Note: Where something is always true we can use *never* or *always* with the imperative.

Always wear a seatbelt when driving. Never drink and drive.

Practice: imperatives

1 Match 1–8 to a–h to make imperatives.

1	Wait for me	a	the wet paint!
2	Don't touch	b	before you leave the office.
3	Cross the street	c	before meals.
4	Save the document	d	when you enter the aeroplane.
5	Take these pills	e	before you shut down the computer.
6	Push this button	f	at the bus stop.
7	Lock your desk	g	when the light is green.
8	Switch off your phone	h	to transfer the call.

2 Gretchen is giving safety instructions to some visitors to her factory. Complete her speech with the verbs in the box.

| follow | keep | put on | stay |
| switch off | take | talk | touch | wear |

'Good morning, everyone! I'm Gretchen and I'll be your guide inside the mill. Before we start, for your safety there are some rules and instructions I need to go over. First of all, please _____ these helmets, safety glasses and safety shoes, and to keep your hands clean please _____ these gloves. When we are in the factory _____ inside the yellow lines and _____ your hands out of your pockets. _____ my instructions at all times and don't _____ any moving parts. If you have any questions, please ask me – don't _____ to the operators. Finally, don't _____ any photographs inside the plant and please _____ all electronic equipment before we go in. Right, please follow me and I'll show you …'

UNIT 9 Grammar reference

Sequencing words

The words *first*, *second*, *third*, etc., *then* and *finally* almost always come at the beginning of a sentence when you are giving instructions.

First, turn on the printer. Then check the ink levels.

Note: a comma is used after *first*, *second*, *third*, and *finally*, but not after *then*.

The words *after (that)* and *next* often come at the beginning of a sentence, but can also come at the end, especially in short sentences.

Next, check the ink levels.
Check the ink levels next.

Note the verb forms required with *before*:

Before turning on *the printer, add the paper.*
*Add the paper **before you turn on** the printer.*

Practice: sequencing words

1 Complete the paragraph with words from the box. One word is not used.

> after that   before   finally   first   second
> then   third

How to use an online storage system

_____, research online to find a storage system you like. Some are free, and some cost money. _____, register for an account. _____, download the software to your computer. Click on the application to open it _____. _____ you upload your files to the online storage folder, make sure you back them up! _____, check to make sure …

2 Write the words in the correct order to make sentences.

1 to / walk / bus stop / first, / the

_____

2 number 27 bus / the / second, / to the city centre / take

_____

3 the station, / transfer to / get to / the number 12 bus / after you

_____

4 you / get off / the big park / the bus before / pass

_____

5 minutes after / five / for about / that / walk west

_____

6 will see / finally / my house / you

_____

134 UNIT 9 Get Ready for International Business

UNIT 10 Grammar reference

Past simple

Use the past simple to talk about a situation in the past, an event or events that took place in the past once, several times, or never.

Situation in the past (not true now)	I worked in Germany for 10 years.
Action that finished in the past	Production increased last year.
Series of actions in the past (completed)	I finished the document, saved it and then printed it before the meeting.

For regular verbs, the past simple ends in -ed (work**ed**, play**ed**, manufactur**ed**, graduat**ed**, continu**ed**). Irregular verbs take a different form (write = wrote, go = went, be = was / were, forget = forgot, take = took, hear = heard). For a list of common irregular verbs, see page 00.

For questions and negatives, use *did* or *didn't* (with *be* use *was/were*).

Did you call the customer?	Yes, I did.	No, I didn't.
Did you finish the report?		
When did exports increase?	Two years ago.	
How was the meeting?	It was good.	
Were the customers busy?	Yes, they were.	No, they weren't.
Was she angry?	Yes, she was.	No, she wasn't.

Practice: past simple

1 Rewrite the sentences using the past simple.

1 I usually arrive at the office before 9 o'clock.
   Yesterday *I arrived at the office before 9 o'clock.*

2 Exports are increasing sharply.
   In 2011 _____.

3 I go to the gym every day.
   Last week _____.

4 I am happy to see you again.
   _____ last night.

5 I study engineering at university.
   From 2008 to 2012 _____.

2 What did you do yesterday? Write some sentences describing what you did.

_____
_____
_____
_____

3 Look at these answers to some questions. Write the questions.

Q. _____?
A. Yes, they were.
Q. _____?
A. Exports increased in 2010.
Q. _____?
A. No, they didn't.
Q. _____?
A. 10 years ago.
Q. _____?
A. Yes, I did.
Q. _____?
A. I gave a presentation, then I talked to some customers.
Q. _____?
A. I worked in Paris for 10 years.

UNIT 11 Grammar reference

will / be going to

Use *will / won't* for offers and promises.

*I'll send you my application. / I **won't** be late.*

Use *will / won't* for quick decisions about the future.

A: It's raining!
B: Oh, then I'll take a taxi.

Use *be going to* for future plans.

We're going to go to New Zealand this summer.

Practice: will / be going to

1 Complete the sentences with the correct form of the verbs in brackets.

1 He _____ finish the reports. (not / going to)
2 There's too much traffic. I _____ be able to get there in time. (not / will)
3 _____ you _____ pack your suitcase tonight? (going to)
4 Promise me you _____ call me when you get there. (will)
5 They said they _____ lower the price. (will / not)
6 They _____ attend the seminar. (not / be going to)

2 Circle the correct answer.

1 A: What are you doing this weekend?
　B: *I'll have / I'm going to have* a tennis lesson.
2 A: Can you get me the sales report?
　B: *I'll get it right away. / I'm going to get it right away.*
3 A: Remember the time difference between here and Sydney.
　B: Oh, that's right. OK, *I won't / I'm not going to* call before 9:00am their time.
4 A: I hear you're transferring to Beijing next year.
　B: Yes, so *I'll take / I'm going to take* a Chinese Mandarin class.
5 A: I can't get this document to print correctly.
　B: Don't worry, *I'll help you / I'm going to help you.*

UNIT 12 Grammar reference

Making and responding to offers

Making offers is a common part of conversation in English. To make an offer, use *Would you like* with a noun or *Would you like / Would you like me* with the infinitive (*to* …).

Would you like	a sandwich? some (more) coffee? to play golf this weekend? to see our new catalogue?
Would you like me to	help you? show you where the room is? carry your bag?

Respond to offers with *Yes, please* or *No, thank you* (we often add a positive comment when accepting an offer, or a reason when refusing).

Yes, please.	I'd love one / some. I'd love to. That would be great.
No, thank you.	I'm fine. I'm sorry, but I can't. I need to work this weekend.

Practice: making and responding to offers

1 Match the offers 1–6 to the responses a–f.

Would you like …

1	some cake?	a	No, thank you. I'm sorry but I can't tomorrow.
2	me to carry that?	b	No, thank you. It's not heavy.
3	to have lunch tomorrow?	c	Yes, please. Which floor is it on?
4	me to send you the report?	d	No, thank you. I'm fine.
5	another cup of coffee?	e	Yes, please. It looks delicious.
6	to see my office?	f	Yes, please. Can you email it to me?

2 Write offers and responses for these situations.

1 Your friend visits your house. It is a hot day and she looks thirsty.
   You: Would you like _____?
   Friend: _____

2 You are sitting on a bus with no empty seats. A young woman gets on the bus carrying a baby.
   You: Would you like _____?
   Woman: _____

3 A foreign businessman is visiting your company. After the meeting he has no plans in the evening.
   You: Would you like _____?
   Visitor: _____

4 You see some tourists looking at a map in front of the train station.
   You: Would you like _____?
   Tourist: _____

Macmillan Education
4 Crinan Street
London N1 9XW
A division of Macmillan Publishers Limited
Companies and representatives throughout the world

ISBN: 978-0-230-43325-0 (TOEIC edition)
ISBN: 978-0-230-44786-8 (BEC edition)

Text © Andrew Vaughan & Dorothy E. Zemach 2013
Design and illustration ©Macmillan Publishers Limited 2013

The authors have asserted their rights to be identified as the authors of this work in accordance with the Copyright, Design and Patents Act 1988

BEC practice material written by Michael Black

First edition published 2008
This edition published 2013

All rights reserved; no part of this publication may be reproduced, stored in a retrieval system, transmitted in any form, or by any means, electronic, mechanical, photocopying, recording, or otherwise, without the prior written permission of the publishers.

Designed by Carolyn Gibson
Page make-up by Carolyn Gibson
Illustrated by Nigel Dobbyn, Peter Harper, Gregory Roberts and Paul Williams
Cover design by Carolyn Gibson
Cover photographs: Getty

Extracts from the *Macmillan English Dictionary* second edition published 2007 © Macmillan Publishers Limited 2007.

The authors wish to extend their thanks to all those who contributed to this book with their generous advice and assistance. We would especially like to thank our colleagues, management, and students (past and present) at Sumitomo Electric Industries, Sumitomo Metal Industries, Sumikin-Intercom, and other companies, for giving us the experience we needed and for trying out many of the ideas in this book.

For assistance with information about international business customs, cross-cultural communication, and the TOEIC: Brett Berquist, Tammy Gilbert, Peiya Gu, Alan Headbloom, Lewis Lansford, Shinji Okumura, Bruce Rogers, Jaimie Scanlon, Tadao Seo, Lynn Stafford-Yilmaz, Kelly Tavares, Gregg Stevens, Kay Westerfield, Tatyana Yahkontova

Thanks to everyone at Macmillan for their support and guidance in the development of this book.

Finally – thanks to our families for their patience and support: Hiroko, Sarah, and Thomas Vaughan; and Will and Sebastian Mitchell.

TOEIC ® is a registered trademark of Educational Testing Service (ETS). This publication is not endorsed or approved by ETS.

BEC (Cambridge English: Business English Certificates) are certificates of attainment in business English awarded by Cambridge English Language Assessment, part of the University of Cambridge. This product is not endorsed or approved by Cambridge English.

The test questions and other testing information herein are provided in their entirety by Macmillan Publishers.

The authors and publishers would like to thank the following for permission to reproduce their photographs: **Alamy Images** p62tl; Alamy/ PanaromaMedia p.47(r); **Art Directors and Trip** p10(tm); **Bananastock** pp16(tl), 16(r), P22(tm), 25(r), 25(l), 27(tm),28(m), 36(tr), 40, 42(tr), 46(l), 62(tm), 68(tm), 80(tr), 112(l), 34(r), 46(r), 80(breakfast), 80(watching TV), 80(party); **Corbis** p114(r); **Digital Vision** pp28(r), 62(tr), 62(r); **Getty Images/Stone/Siri Stafford** p80tl; **Image Source** pp10(tl), 10(tr), P22(tr), 16(tm), 36(tm), 42(tl), 42(tm), 47(l), 54(tm), 54(tr), 68(tl), 68(tr), 108(l), 110(l), 110(r), 112(r), 114(l); 116(r) 118(r), 22(br), 34(l), 80(sports); **istock/Tatian popova** p8; **Photodisc** p99; **Photolibrary.com** p28(tl); **Photoalto** p87; **Punchstock** pp22(bm), P22(tl), 80(tm); 80(dessert), 80(unhappy), 81; **Stockbyte** pp22(bl), 108(r), 116(l), 118(l); **Thinkstock** pp36(tl), 54(tl).

References to photographs on pages 108-119 refer to the TOEIC edition.

Although we have tried to trace and contact copyright holders before publication, in some cases this has not been possible. If contacted we will be pleased to rectify any errors or omissions at the earliest opportunity.

These materials may contain links for third party websites. We have no control over, and are not responsible for, the contents of such third party websites. Please use care when accessing them.

Printed and bound in Thailand
2020 2019 2018 2017
14 13 12 11 10 9